MW00489720

Reading this book made me want to start an adoption support group that very day! Sprinkled with encouraging stories and packed with detailed, step-by-step ideas, this practical tool will unleash God's help and hope and release the gifts of His people.

Kristin Swick Wong,
author of *Carried Safely Home:*
The Spiritual Legacy of an Adoptive Family

If I were to start an adoption ministry tomorrow, this is one of the first books I would grab. If you care about adoption and believe your church can help, you need this indispensable resource.

Christopher Padbury,
Executive Director, Colorado's Project 1.27, and
adoptive dad of five

With this book as a guide, creating an adoption ministry just became much simpler. Worksheets included throughout the book provide an opportunity for real-life application. An incredible resource for anyone considering starting an adoption support ministry.

Julie Donahue,
Co-Founder and Director Emeritus of
Hannah's Prayer Ministries,
and mom by both birth and adoption

Includes *all* the essentials needed to start an adoption community of support. As a pastor, adoptive dad, and believer in miracles, I urge you to get this informative, inspiring guide, and use it!

Ray Moore,
Pastor of Congregational Care, University
Presbyterian Church, Seattle, Washington

If you know anyone struggling with infertility or adoption issues, this book offers a quick primer to help you understand their world. You'll be glad you read it—and so will they.

Pat J. Sikora,
author of *Why Didn't You Warn Me?*
How to Deal With Challenging Group Members

Through personal experience and extensive research, Laura Christianson has written a book that answers the questions of those desiring to lock arms with others traveling the adoption journey. Practical "how-tos" combined with real life stories make this step-by-step guide one you will refer to time and time again.

Sharon Jaynes,
international speaker and author of eleven books, including *Being a Great Mom-Raising Great Kids, Becoming the Woman of His Dreams, Building an Effective Women's Ministry,* and *Experience the Ultimate Makeover*

The ADOPTION NETWORK

Your Guide to Starting a Support System

LAURA CHRISTIANSON
Author of *The Adoption Decision*

WINEPRESS WP PUBLISHING

© 2007 by Laura Christianson. All rights reserved.

WinePress Publishing (PO Box 428, Enumclaw, WA 98022) functions only as book publisher. As such, the ultimate design, content, editorial accuracy, and views expressed or implied in this work are those of the author.

No part of this publication may be reproduced, stored in a retrieval system or transmitted in any way by any means—electronic, mechanical, photocopy, recording or otherwise—without the prior permission of the copyright holder, except as provided by USA copyright law.

Unless otherwise noted, all Scriptures are taken from the Holy Bible, New International Version, Copyright © 1973, 1978, 1984 by the International Bible Society. Used by permission of Zondervan Publishing House. The "NIV" and "New International Version" trademarks are registered in the United States Patent and Trademark Office by International Bible Society.

Scripture references marked NLT are taken from the Holy Bible, New Living Translation, copyright © 1996 by Tyndale Charitable Trust. Used by permission of Tyndale House Publishers, Wheaton, Illinois 60189. All rights reserved.

Scripture references marked NRSV are taken from the New Revised Standard Version of the Bible, copyright © 1989 by the Division of Christian Education of the National Council of Churches of Christ in the United States of America. Used by permission.

Scripture references marked MSG are taken from The Message Bible © 1993 by Eugene N. Peterson, NavPress, POB 35001, Colorado Springs, CO 80935, 4th printing in USA 1994. Published in association with the literary agency—Aline Comm. POB 49068, Colorado Springs, CO 80949. Used by permission.

ISBN 13: 978-1-57921-902-4
ISBN 10: 1-57921-902-0
Library of Congress Catalog Card Number: 2007922661

Now to him who is able to do immeasurably more than all we ask or imagine, according to his power that is at work within us, to him be glory in the church and in Christ Jesus throughout all generations, for ever and ever.

—Ephesians 3:20–21

CONTENTS

Acknowledgments

I'm grateful for the many people whose thoughts, inspiration, and guidance played a role in bringing this book to fruition:

Julie Donahue: You sparked my interest in adoption ministry over a decade ago when you launched Ladies in Waiting, a Christian Internet support group for moms-in-waiting.

Ray Moore, pastor of Congregational Care at University Presbyterian Church in Seattle: I'm grateful for your invaluable assistance in developing Heartbeat Ministries. To the Heartbeat Ministries' leaders and participants: You are the most loving, giving people anyone could hope to work with.

Timothy and Carla Williams and Athena Dean: You are such a gift to me! I cherish your friendship, your enthusiasm, and your unwavering commitment to this project. It is a delight to partner with you and the rest of the WinePress gang.

George Dillaway and Josiah Williams: Thanks for contributing your amazing artistic and organizational talents during the book's production.

Kari Brodin, Lynn Crooks, Jenn Doucette, Paul Gossard, Jenna Hatfield, Janet McElvaine, Steve Miller, and Christopher Padbury: I appreciate your sage advice and thoughtful critiques.

Gerald D. Clark and Johnston H. Moore: Your insights expanded my vision of adoption ministry.

Robert (my dear hubby), and Ben and Josh (my cherished sons): Thanks for your ongoing support of my writing ventures, and particularly, for sustaining me with mochas. I love you guys!

Introduction

had just settled into my seat before the worship service when I felt a tap on my shoulder. The friend sitting behind me pointed across the aisle and whispered, "See that woman over there? She's having difficulty getting pregnant. You should meet her."

Sounds like an odd comment until you consider I started a ministry for infertile couples and prospective adoptive parents at my church. I had become known as the 'go-to' person for would-be parents in need of encouragement.

My husband and I are lifetime members of The Club No One Wants To Join—a.k.a.—The Infertility Club. We're also adoptive parents twice over. During the years Robert and I struggled with fertility challenges, we also struggled with the reactions of those around us. Friends asked why we were still childless after 10 years of marriage. Relatives advised us to "get busy." People from church, assuming we needed something to occupy our time, "volunteered" us to lead the youth group and babysit in the nursery.

Few verbalized the words we longed to hear: "I'm sorry you're going through this. How can I support you?"

When Robert and I began exploring the possibility of adopting, the scenario didn't change much. Friends warned us adopting a child could take years. Relatives worried about birth parents who might want their child back. And most people from church didn't even know we were adopting. Wary our church friends would regale us with horror stories of adoptions gone wrong, we didn't announce our plan to adopt.

During our journey to adoption, few verbalized the words we longed to hear: "Congratulations! I'm excited you're becoming parents. How can I support you?"

I know now that our relatives, friends, and church family did want to support us. But adoption was a new phenomenon for them; they simply didn't know *how* to support us. And because adoption was new for Robert and me, we didn't know how to ask for support.

During the past decade, I've met countless people who've fought the silent battle of infertility, miscarriage, or infant loss. I've talked with adoptive parents who've endured an interminable "pregnancy" during which they've received little or no encouragement. I've seen women and men who relinquish a child for adoption shed silent tears of anguish. I've encountered adopted people of all ages who silently yearn to know their birth parents, fearful that initiating a search will offend their adoptive family.

"If only I had another person to talk with who understands what I'm going through," they tell me. "It would make all the difference."

As Robert and I progressed through two adoptions, God developed in me a deep compassion towards those who experience fertility challenges or are considering adoption. I sensed God's "still, small voice" nudging me to reach out to others who were waiting for a child.

The nudge became a shove when we moved to Seattle, Washington. Robert and I and our two young sons left our rural church of 100 members and began attending University Presbyterian, an urban church that has a larger population than the town from which we moved. Each Sunday, I scoured the announcements, looking for ways to connect with others. There were small groups for first-time moms, social events for parents of preschoolers, and Bible studies for men, women, and couples. Only one group was missing: a group for those who were waiting to become parents.

Convinced there must be several adoptive moms in our congregation of 4,000, I sidled up to Caucasian couples who had Asian or African American children in tow. "Are you an adoptive parent?" I queried. "So am I. Want to start a small group?"

Three adoptive moms agreed to help brainstorm ways our church could minister to infertile couples and adoptive families. We shared our ideas with our pastor, and in 1998, Heartbeat Ministries was conceived.

Although our church staff was enthusiastic about the possibilities for an infertility and adoption ministry, they cautioned us that not many people would be interested. Today, those same staff members marvel that Heartbeat Ministries has served close to 200 families in the Seattle area.

The primary mission of our all-volunteer ministry is to "hold people's hearts"—to equip and encourage those who wait for a child through birth or adoption. We do that through providing a resource lending library, an Internet discussion group, one-to-one mentoring, workshops, seminars, and support groups.

In addition to supporting families who are waiting for a child, we help those in our faith community develop awareness of the unique challenges infertile couples and adoptive families face. As word of our ministry has spread, we've had the joy of helping other churches launch infertility and/or adoption ministries.

While our church's support network serves infertile couples as well as adoptive families, many people who adopt do not experience fertility challenges. You can adapt the information in this handbook for use with infertility support groups, but the book's primary emphasis is on building adoption support networks.

Whether you're a layperson or a pastor, this guidebook will challenge you to "think outside the box" as you strategize. The worksheets in each chapter walk you step-by-step through the "nuts and bolts" of planning a faith-based network for parents-in-waiting, adoptive families, birth/first parents, adopted people, and foster parents.

My hope and prayer is that the resources in *The Adoption Network* will inspire and equip you as you follow God's call to minister to those touched by adoption. As others catch your vision, you'll discover untold ways in which in your church and community can make a lasting impact in the life of a birth parent, an adoptive parent, and most importantly—a child.

Chapter One

The Need for Adoption Support Networks

And what does the Lord require of you? To act justly and to love mercy and to walk humbly with your God.

—Micah 6:8

Renee Carver* longed for someone—anyone—to reach out to her during the time she and her husband were waiting to adopt their daughter. "There were older women in my church who had adopted years ago. But they never approached me," says Renee. "I feel our pastor should have asked them to actively support me. I think everyone was just afraid to bring it up."

Some church leaders even discourage those who build families through adoption. When Janice and Carl Wilson,* parents of seven children through birth and adoption, told their pastor they planned to adopt another child, he cautioned, "Your desire to adopt is bordering on unhealthy."

Janice and Carl nervously laughed off their pastor's comment. But later, they realized how much it bothered them. It bothered them so much, in fact, that they left their church. "Of all the places you're supposed to count on for support, it's from your church," says Janice.

While many secular resources and support groups are available for adoptive families and birth parents, faith communi-

---

* Names have been changed

ties tend to ignore, rather than support, those considering adoption.

Some church leaders assume there aren't enough people in their congregations with a stake in adoption to warrant ministering to them. Statistics prove otherwise; adoptive families represent a fast-growing segment of the population:

- Approximately 1 million U.S. families actively seek adoption at any given time.[1]
- Each year, from 130,000 to 150,000 adoptions are approved in U.S. courts.[2]
- International adoptions have more than doubled in the last decade, as have adoptions through foster care.[3]
- One-third of all Americans are touched by adoption within their immediate families.[4]
- Sixty-five percent of Americans have experience with adoption through family or close friends, meaning a family member or a close friend was adopted, adopted a child, or relinquished a child for adoption.[5]

Considering the average attendance at a Protestant church is 124,[6] we can deduce that 41 people in a typical congregation have direct ties to adoption.

Adoption's emotional price tag is high. Those seeking to become foster or adoptive parents submit to a rigorous screening process that includes answering intimate, probing questions intended to determine their parenting potential. Once approved to adopt, parents-to-be anxiously await the child they hope will someday be theirs.

Women who experience an unplanned pregnancy weigh the pros and cons of parenting versus planning for their child's adoption. They, too, anxiously anticipate making the decision that will irrevocably change the course of several lives.

The faith community has a responsibility and a biblical mandate to minister to adoptive and foster families and to care for orphans.[7] That means providing for the orphans themselves as well as supporting those who provide homes for orphans, foster children, and other youngsters who need a family.

The faith community must also minister to women who experience unplanned pregnancy. Many women who get pregnant unexpectedly are Christians who attend Bible-believing churches. Yet, when a woman from within the church acknowledges her unintentional pregnancy, some point accusatory fingers at the "sinner" (and her partner). Rather than condemning these women, the church family should enfold them with forgiveness and friendship.

In his letter to the church at Ephesus, the apostle Paul writes that God "destined us for adoption as his children through Jesus Christ."[8] The lives of all who invite Jesus to be their Savior are transformed through spiritual adoption into God's family.

All Christians enjoy an eternal legacy as God's adopted children. And God calls His children to affirm one another in love and carry each other's burdens.[9] There's no better way to respond to that call than to minister to those in our churches and communities whose lives are impacted by adoption.

Chapter Two

Types of Adoption
Support Networks

There are different kinds of spiritual gifts, but the same Spirit is the source of them all. There are different kinds of service, but we serve the same Lord.
                                        —1 Corinthians 12:4–5 (NLT)

had just completed teaching a five-week series of "Exploring Adoption" workshops at my church. One participant, who listened with rapt attention and furiously scribbled notes during every session, approached me after class. "You're like a walking encyclopedia of adoption," she marveled.

My new friend used the information she gleaned from the workshops to jump-start her own adoption plan. She and several other women who attended that workshop series formed a support group for singles who were waiting to adopt. Those ten women loved each other through mountains of governmental red tape, multiple failed foster and adoptive placements, and finally, the successful adoption of more than a dozen children.

The group eventually morphed into an informal social group for single adoptive moms and their toddlers. During our most recent "Exploring Adoption" series, several of those women— now walking encyclopedias of adoption themselves—shared their experiences and expertise.

Discovering the diversity that exists among those interested in adoption is one of the many rewards of launching an adoption support network. Finding ways to meet the needs of those who participate in your network and equipping them to reach out to others is equally rewarding. As you prayerfully consider how your adoption network will "look," consider the following people to whom you might minister:

People considering adoption. Those who haven't decided whether adoption is the right option for them have different needs than those actively involved in the process. Adoption novices often don't know the first thing about adoption, but they're eager to learn. They appreciate workshops that introduce them to different types of adoption and they like collecting resource materials to peruse at their leisure.

Couples transitioning from infertility to adoption. Before they're emotionally ready to adopt, infertile couples must work through the grief that accompanies an inability to conceive or carry a child to term. They benefit from therapy-style seminars in which a grief and loss counselor shares techniques for managing infertility. Short-term support groups further help them process emotions and prepare them to build a family through adoption.

People waiting to adopt a child. The adoption process is fraught with anxiety. Parents adopting newborns domestically worry whether they'll be "chosen" by a pregnant woman who wants to place her child with them. They wonder whether the expectant mother will elect to parent, either before or after relinquishing her child.

Parents adopting internationally wonder whether their country of choice will suddenly close its doors to adoption. They worry about the health of their child.

Likewise, foster parents who are planning to adopt fret over governmental bureaucracy, delays, and frustrating visits with their foster child's birth family.

Parents-to-be benefit from waiting parent support groups. These groups often re-invent themselves as new parent support groups, adoptive family social groups, play groups, or small groups that encompass specific subsets of adoption: open, closed, foster-adopt, single parent, international, or special needs.

Foster parents. In order to maintain their license, foster parents adhere to stringent requirements. They parent children scarred by neglect or abuse and they willingly facilitate reunification efforts among children and their birth families. Because their social workers carry overwhelming caseloads, foster parents rely on others within the foster parenting network for information, advice, and encouragement.

Foster parents require (and deserve) respite care—for their children and for themselves. Imagine how they would value the support of others who become licensed foster parents for the sole purpose of providing respite care.

People whose adoptions fail. When an anticipated adoption falls through the cracks, the grieving almost-parents covet nonjudgmental listening, one-to-one mentoring, and ongoing prayer support.

Parents of infants and toddlers. New parents love to recommend their favorite pediatricians and pre-schools to fellow parents. They commiserate about potty training and delight in their child's first words and first steps. But adoptive parents can feel like outsiders in groups where the chatter revolves around pregnancy and childbirth. They appreciate parenting classes, social groups, play groups, or support groups where they can re-tell their adoption story, share the joys and challenges of parenting, and discuss issues pertinent to adoptive families.

Parents whose children face unique challenges. When people begin parenting foster and adopted children, they often discover challenges they feel unprepared to tackle: diseases, physical disabilities, attachment issues, psychotic disorders, or trauma stemming from neglect, abuse, or institutionalization. Needs-based support groups help parents navigate specific challenges with others who understand those issues.

People experiencing an unplanned pregnancy. Women and their partners need a safe, supportive environment in which to carefully consider the short- and long-term ramifications of parenting versus placing their child for adoption. They appreciate one-to-one mentoring and referrals to pregnancy counselors who will assist them as they plan for their child's future. Many pregnant women are also in need of maternity clothing, housing, and rides to appointments.

People who have relinquished a child for adoption. Whether they released a child for adoption recently or years ago, birth/ first parents value non-judgmental listening, mentoring, and prayer support. Support groups can be a highly-effective means of helping birth parents work through sadness, anger, fear, uncertainty about their child's well-being, and other issues that accompany placing a child for adoption.

Biological grandparents of children placed for adoption. Birth grandparents are perhaps the most powerless people involved in an adoption. When their daughter or son experiences an unplanned pregnancy, the grandparents-to-be wonder, "What did I do wrong?"

While they often wield substantial influence in their daughter or son's decision to place a child for adoption, they do not make the final decision. And if their daughter or son opts for a closed adoption, the grandparents face the likelihood they will not get to know their grandchild. Confused, hurt, and angry, biological grandparents crave the listening ear of others who have been in their shoes.

People seeking to reunite with a child they placed for adoption or with a birth family member. Birth parents and the children they placed for adoption do not forget one another. Those in closed or international adoptions, who possess little or no information about each other, may develop intense feelings of longing for one another. They appreciate support groups, counseling, and information about no-cost and low-cost adoption search and reunion registries.

People who work at pregnancy resource centers. Women who visit crisis pregnancy centers are often offered two alternatives: abortion or parenting. Specialized training for counselors at these centers may spur them to present adoption as an option for their clients.

Adopted children. Children enjoy exploring their ethnic, cultural, and adoptive heritage. As children enter the 'tween and teen years, they become more aware of adoption prejudice and begin working through personal adoption issues. They benefit from interacting with others who were adopted. Culture camps, play groups, social groups, workshops, and support groups help adopted children and their families broaden their world view and meet others who have a similar background.

Emancipated foster children. More than 20,000 teenagers "age out" of foster care each year, but they still need families. Foster parents sometimes adopt their former foster children; one man was adopted on his 21st birthday. Another woman was legally adopted at age 41 by a woman she'd known when she lived in foster care. Supporting or adopting an emancipated person provides a sense of stability, love, and a permanent family for someone who has never had one.

Adopted adults. Adoption-related identity issues surface during adolescence and into adulthood. Support groups, workshops, and mentoring help adopted adults express, process, and resolve emotional upheaval.

Pastors and lay leaders who seek training in adoption ministry. While church leaders are empathetic and caring, many are unfamiliar with the unique challenges adoption presents. They appreciate workshops, presentations, and discussions that acquaint them with adoption terminology, the adoption process, adoption-related issues, and orphan/waiting child ministry.

Church leaders who catch the vision for adoption ministry become powerful influencers of others in their churches and communities.

The faith community. Church members and attendees need instruction about how to emotionally and/or financially support those in the congregation who are adopting or placing a child for adoption. They are most motivated to act after listening to presentations about adoption during the worship service, during a Sunday school class, or during a conference or meeting.

An adoption support network doesn't have to be large; your network might consist of two people who meet regularly to chat informally about adoption. And that's okay. Oftentimes, the deepest sharing and healing occurs within intimate groups. Whether two people or two hundred people show up, your group will be successful as long as you're committed to one another.

WORKSHEET
TARGETING THE AUDIENCE FOR YOUR SUPPORT NETWORK

Check the group(s) you would most like to reach:

- ☐ People beginning to explore the idea of adopting a child
- ☐ Couples transitioning from infertility to adoption
- ☐ People who are waiting to adopt a child
- ☐ Foster parents who are planning to adopt
- ☐ Foster parents
- ☐ People whose adoptions fail
- ☐ Parents of infants and toddlers
- ☐ Parents whose children face unique challenges
- ☐ People experiencing an unplanned pregnancy
- ☐ People who have relinquished a child for adoption
- ☐ Biological grandparents of children placed for adoption
- ☐ People seeking to be reunited with a child they placed for adoption or with a birth family member
- ☐ People who work at pregnancy resource centers
- ☐ Adopted children
- ☐ Emancipated foster children
- ☐ Adopted adults
- ☐ Pastors and lay leaders who seek training in adoption ministry
- ☐ The faith community
- ☐ Other _____

Mix and match the groups listed in the previous question. Try combining several of the groups (for example, your network could encompass couples transitioning from infertility, people beginning to explore the idea of adopting, and those waiting to adopt). Which combinations work best?

WORKSHEET
TARGETING THE AUDIENCE FOR YOUR
SUPPORT NETWORK

Which combinations do you want to avoid?

Survey your constituency to find out what their needs are. List the top three needs:

1.

2.

3.

Ask those you survey to recommend people connected to adoption and people interested in learning more about it.

Contact local adoption and foster care organizations and adoption professionals. Ask them what types of groups they feel are needed in your community. Ask them to recommend people who are looking to lead or join an adoption network.

Chapter Three

How to Organize
Your Network

O God, who has bound us together in this bundle of life, give us grace to understand how our lives depend upon the courage, the industry, the honesty, and the integrity of our fellow human beings; that we may be mindful of their needs, grateful for their faithfulness, and faithful in our responsibilities to them; through Jesus Christ our Lord.
        —Reinhold Niebuhr, theologian (1892–1971)

When I told my pastor I wanted to start an adoption ministry, he advised me, "Write a mission statement and then we'll talk more." At first I assumed his advice was a ploy to ascertain my commitment to launching a new ministry. I grudgingly agreed to draft a mission statement, assuming it would wend its way through umpteen committees before being approved.

   As our planning team began brainstorming, we discovered our pastor had given us sound advice. Writing a mission statement helped us define and refine our vision and goals and gave us something concrete to present to our church's decision-makers. In addition to developing a mission statement, we also solicited pastoral support, planned a budget, and recruited leadership before launching our ministry.

DEVELOPING A MISSION STATEMENT

A mission statement defines your group's core purpose. This brief statement explains:

1. Who you are
2. What you do
3. How you serve

If you've never written a mission statement, visit Web sites (particularly non-profit and church sites) and read their mission statements to get a feel for how they are worded. If you're starting a church-based adoption network, read your church's mission statement and closely align your ministry's statement with it.

As your network grows and changes, you'll tweak your mission statement. Refer to it regularly; it will keep you focused on the critical areas in which you're committed to serve.

The Heartbeat Ministries mission statement is prefaced with an explanation of our name:

> The name "Heartbeat" symbolizes our hope to create a family. We believe that, to God, all our heartbeats sound the same, whether our families are "homegrown," are created by assisted reproductive technology, or are born in our hearts through adoption.

A succinct, memorable statement explains the unique nature of the ministry:

> Our mission is to hold people's hearts—to provide hope and healing based on God's Word and on His unfailing love.

The *Adoption Network*

We further define our mission with three goal statements:

Recognizing that God calls us to support and affirm one another in love (John 15:17), and to carry each other's burdens (Galatians 6:2), we:

1. Nurture and support those who are waiting for a child through birth or adoption.
2. Provide opportunities for infertile couples and adoptive families to meet, socialize, and discuss issues in a Christian setting.
3. Educate the church family about the unique challenges infertile couples and adoptive families face.

Immediately following our mission and goal statements, we provide information about our leadership and our ministry partner:

Our volunteer leaders are Christian men and women who have experienced fertility challenges and/or adoption. Several of our leaders are medical professionals, social workers, or adoption attorneys. All Heartbeat events are open to the public. We welcome anyone who desires to attend.

Heartbeat Ministries is a ministry of University Presbyterian Church, 4540 Fifteenth Avenue NE, Seattle, Washington 98105, 206-524-7300.

WORKSHEET
DEVELOPING A MISSION STATEMENT

Sum up the purpose of your support network in one word:

In three words:

    1.

    2.

    3.

List the primary people your network will serve:

List any groups your network will not serve (some adoption networks exclude singles or same-sex couples. Others serve birth mothers but not birth fathers. Still others serve foster parents but not adoptive parents):

If your network will be faith-based, state your guiding biblical principles. List Scripture verse(s) that capture your ministry's "flavor":

WORKSHEET
DEVELOPING A MISSION STATEMENT

List your short-term and long-term goals:

Next 9 months:

Next 2-to-3 years:

Summarize your network's key mission in 25 words or less:

Brainstorm simple, attention-grabbing names for your network:

Describe your leadership:

Describe your group's sponsorship and list contact information:

SOLICITING SUPPORT

When I proposed launching an adoption ministry to my pastor, I had no idea of what to expect. New to my church, I had never met this particular pastor (I attend a large church with multiple pastors). But my life motto is, "It never hurts to ask," so I did just that.

Of course, I didn't go into our meeting "cold"—I prepared a detailed proposal to review with him. My pastor—an adoptive dad himself—was thrilled I wanted to start a ministry for adoptive families and immediately offered his support. I left his office grinning, delighted he'd been so receptive to my ideas.

If you're starting a church-based adoption network, you'll need to determine where your ministry will fit within the church structure. Departments that offer a comfortable fit for an adoption ministry include:

- Small Groups
- Christian Education
- Care and Support Ministries
- Marriage/Family Ministries
- Children's Ministries
- Women's Ministries
- Community Life
- Prayer Ministries

You'll also need approval from your pastoral staff and/or your church's governing body. If you attend a small church, you'll likely present your proposal to your senior pastor first. If you attend a large church, you'll meet with the pastor/director of a particular department.

Obtaining backing from your church leadership is the single most important action you should take before launching your group. Once you have their enthusiastic support, your pastoral leaders will help guide and grow your group among the congregation and throughout your community.

WORKSHEET
MEETING WITH THE DECISION-MAKERS

During your first meeting with your adoption network's prospective ministry partner, do the following:

- Share your adoption story and explain your passion for this type of ministry.
- Explain your qualifications for coordinating the group.
- Review pertinent adoption statistics (see Chapter 1).
- Explain how an adoption network will benefit individuals within the sponsoring organization and the organization as a whole (you may have to do some convincing here, especially if the decision-maker has little or no experience with adoption).
- If your network will be faith-based, explain the biblical foundation for your ministry.
- Explain how your mission complements or enhances the organization's overall mission and meets a need that's not currently being addressed.
  - Discuss whether you'll minister primarily to individuals or groups. If you focus on groups, will they be small (6 to 12 people), medium (30 people), or large (over 100 people)?
  - Discuss whether your events will be instruction-oriented, counseling-oriented, or a combination.
  - Discuss whether your ministry will reach out to the community, encourage those within the church, or both.[10]
- Provide the decision-maker with testimonials from people who support your mission.
- If you meet with your pastor or a decision-maker from a faith-based organization, pray together. Seek God's guidance as you collaborate on birthing a new ministry.

WORKSHEET
MEETING WITH THE DECISION-MAKERS

- ✐ Print multiple copies of your proposal and give them to the decision-maker.
- ✐ Schedule a follow-up meeting for no later than one month after your first meeting. A one-month gap gives the decision-maker time to circulate your proposal, but doesn't allow him or her enough time to forget about you.

During your second meeting with your adoption network's prospective ministry partner, do the following:

- ✐ Discuss input the decision-maker has received regarding your proposal.
- ✐ Refine your mission statement.
- ✐ Review your preliminary budget, negotiating areas in which you can tweak the budget.
- ✐ Discuss potential meeting locations for your events. If you plan to meet at your church, review the church calendar together to determine optimal dates, times, and room availability.

Before your new ministry is approved, you may be asked to present your proposal to your church's governing body or to an organization's board of directors. During that meeting, you'll review the pertinent points of your proposal in front of a larger group. If the thought of making a presentation panics you, tell your decision-maker in advance so he or she can assist you.

PLANNING A BUDGET

Most adoption support networks start out as low-budget operations that require little overhead. Heartbeat Ministries, for example, is an all-volunteer network; even the adoption professionals who speak at our workshops volunteer their time. Our participants donate gently-used books for our resource library or they purchase new books and donate them to the church library. Others donate funds to help support the ministry. Our main expense is photocopying workshop materials.

Your network's scope will likely hinge on your budget. If no organization sponsors you, you'll pay expenses out-of-pocket, solicit donations from local businesses and non-profits, or conduct fund-raisers.

If an organization such as a church sponsors you, they may allocate $50, $500, or $5,000 per year. Because sponsoring organizations write you into their budget, you'll need to learn when funds will become available—some organizations won't release funds until the following fiscal year.

Consider soliciting targeted donations from church members or from community groups, individuals, or corporations that support adoption-related causes. Be aware that many corporations require the groups they sponsor to have non-profit status (for information on creating a non-profit 501 (c)(3) corporation, see the *Shaohannah's Hope Foundation* entry in the Appendix). Maintain meticulous records of donations and expenses for tax purposes.

WORKSHEET
PLANNING A BUDGET

Will your adoption support network require a Web site, or will your sponsor provide a page for your group on its Web site?

If you need a Web site, estimate the monthly costs and the total cost for the site's design, development, hosting, and upkeep:

Design:

Development:

Hosting:

Upkeep:

List other components of your group's online presence (see Chapter 4, "The Online Connection"). Estimate the costs for hosting and maintaining each:

Estimate the cost per month for long-distance phone calls:

Will you be sending announcements, flyers, postcards, newsletters, or direct mail advertising via postal mail? If so, estimate the costs for the following items:

WORKSHEET
PLANNING A BUDGET

- ☐ Paper
- ☐ Software
- ☐ Professional design
- ☐ Photocopying/printing (see "Recommended Web Sites" in Appendix for low-cost print services)
- ☐ Ink/toner cartridges
- ☐ Envelopes
- ☐ Labels
- ☐ Postage
- ☐ Mail management services

Will you advertise your network in any of the following:

- ☐ Local newspapers
- ☐ Regional parenting magazines
- ☐ Publications distributed by adoption organizations
- ☐ Adoption agencies, facilitators, and adoption attorneys' offices
- ☐ Sponsoring organization's publication(s)

Estimate the costs for purchasing ads:

What specifications does each publication require (professional design, camera-ready copy, color separation, etc.):

WORKSHEET
PLANNING A BUDGET

Will you need to photocopy materials? If so, can you use your sponsor's copy machine? List photocopying fees:

Does your sponsor outsource print jobs? Or will you photocopy materials at a local print shop? Estimate the costs for your preferred method of printing:

Will you need to rent facilities in which to host meetings, or can you use a room at your sponsor's facility? If so, are you expected to contribute a facility-use fee?

Will you provide refreshments during your events?

Will your sponsoring organization provide items such as coffee and tea, cups, sugar, creamer, and napkins, or will volunteers supply all beverages, food, and utensils?

Will you pay speakers an honorarium or purchase gifts for them? If so, what is the estimated cost?

WORKSHEET
PLANNING A BUDGET

Is any special training needed for your network's leaders? List training venues and fees for each:

Will you purchase books, magazines, etc. for an adoption resource library?

- Will you purchase new or used books?
- How many books/magazine subscriptions do you intend to purchase in order to launch your network?
- How many books/magazines do you intend to purchase each year?
- What is the average cost of the reading materials you intend to purchase?
- Can your sponsor purchase books using a library rate or other discount?
- If your church has a library, can money from the library budget be allocated toward the purchase of books for your group?
- If your network is under the umbrella of a particular ministry within your church, will that ministry allocate budget resources toward the purchase of books?

The *Adoption Network*

RECRUITING LEADERSHIP

Once your adoption support network has been approved, you're on your way! If you haven't already begun recruiting, it's time to seek out like-minded people to co-lead or assist with various aspects of the ministry.

But what if you live in a small community where you're the only person with firsthand adoption experience? Granted, that will make recruiting leaders more challenging. But plenty of people have compassionate hearts and if asked, will play a supportive role in your network.

Is someone in your community a psychotherapist or Christian counselor? That person can help set up a mentoring program or facilitate a discussion about grief and loss issues.

Are you acquainted with a prayer warrior? That person can maintain an e-mail prayer chain for your group.

Do you know a pediatrician or a nurse? That person can speak with your group about adoption medicine or infant care.

Do you have a friend who loves to bake? That person can provide home-baked goodies for an event.

Do you know a teenager who's looking for babysitting jobs? That person can provide childcare during your group's meetings.

Do you know someone who has superb organizational skills? That person can create bibliographies of adoption-related resources for your lending library.

Do you know a techno-whiz? That person can create a Web site, discussion board, or chat room.

Do you know a travel agent? That person can book adoption travel for a discounted fee.

Do you know an interpreter? That person can provide language lessons to parents traveling internationally to adopt, or can interpret for the new family once they return home.

Do you know an adoption attorney? That person can provide discounted adoption services for your group's participants.

Do you know an adoption social worker? That person can teach about foster parenting, the adoption home study process, or a wide range of other adoption-related issues.

Do you know a teacher? That person can share how to create an adoption-friendly classroom or can train others how to teach children with special needs.

Do you know someone who loves to chat on the phone? That person can call adoption agencies to request information packets for the prospective adoptive parents who attend your meetings.

The keys to enlisting leadership are prayer and boldness.

> "Commit your way to the Lord; trust in Him and He will make your righteousness shine like the dawn, the justice of your cause like the noonday sun."[11]

As you pray specifically and expectantly, God will bring to mind energetic, committed people with the exact skills you need to effectively launch and run your network. People seek out volunteer opportunities that enrich them personally and offer them a chance to "give back." Some of these people will initiate contact with you, but most—even those who long to be part of your leadership team—are reluctant to volunteer. However, if you ask them directly, many people say "yes."

After prayerfully considering whom God would have you invite to join the leadership team, approach prospective leaders face-to-face. Explain your mission. Suggest a specific task or job description you have in mind for them and explain why you think they'd be a perfect fit for this ministry (when people believe they'll play a critical role in your network, they're more likely to say "yes"). Ask them to prayerfully consider whether they would like to participate.

While your support network will have a point person or coordinator, a committed leadership team is essential. When several people share ownership, the ministry is buoyed with a wave of energy one person can't generate as effectively. Distributing the responsibilities among several people also alleviates leader burnout.

Remember, God is the single most integral member of your leadership team. "The one who calls you is faithful and he will do it."[12]

WORKSHEET
RECRUITING LEADERSHIP

✍ List the names of people you will contact to request prayer support. Ask them to pray that God would stir the hearts of the people He wants to serve on the leadership team.

✍ Contact local adoption professionals to inquire whether any of their clients have expressed an interest in being involved in an adoption support network.

✍ Ask your group's sponsor to recommend people who might lead, train leaders, or assist with various facets of your network.

✍ Create job descriptions for each member of the leadership team. Here are several possible job titles:
- Ministry Coordinator/Director
- Support Group Leader
- Workshop Director
- Events Coordinator
- Financial Manager
- Resource Librarian
- Mentoring Program Facilitator
- Webmaster
- Prayer Team Coordinator
- Education Specialist
- Public Relations Manager
- Hospitality Host(ess)

Chapter Four

Components of Adoption Support Networks

I thank you, O God, for delivering me from a way of life bound by impossibilities into one that burgeons with opportunities. I will no longer live timidly and cautiously, inhibited by the enemy, but confidently and valiantly, believing in a victorious Jesus Christ.
—Eugene Peterson, pastor, scholar, author, and poet

Most adoption networks start small and grow as people catch the vision. At Heartbeat Ministries, our first goal was to provide accessible information for those experiencing fertility challenges or considering adoption. After creating a resource library, we began offering seminars, workshops, support groups, and mentoring.

RESOURCE LIBRARY

People investigating adoption devour everything they can get their hands on about the topic. While Web sites, Internet discussion forums, and blogs provide abundant information, many people prefer to snuggle up with a book. But bookstores and public libraries carry only a handful of adoption books. Your network's adoption library will be an invaluable resource.

If your budget doesn't warrant purchasing books, prepare annotated bibliographies of recommended resources, instead. At Heartbeat Ministries, we created topical bibliographies, each containing a short description of recommended books/magazines/newsletters. We printed multiple copies of each bibliography and placed them in three-ring binders that we display on a shelf in our church library. We invite people to browse through the binders and take whatever resources interest them. We also filled binders with adoption- and infertility-related magazines, organizations, and newsletters (including newsletters from area adoption agencies).

Suggested Bibliography Topics

- Adopted children
- Adoptive parents
- Birth/first parents
- Fostering and foster-to-adopt
- Infertility issues
- International adoption
- Miscarriage and infant death
- Online resources
- Open adoption
- Special needs adoption

Our church librarian assigned our ministry a shelf in the library and allotted us some budget dollars to purchase books. To make our books easily identifiable, we created a ministry logo which we attach to the spine of all Heartbeat Ministries books. We invite people to check out our books on the honor system so if they wish to remain anonymous, they can borrow a book without officially checking it out.

Our church library is open to the community, so books disappear on a regular basis. While we're delighted people are reading the materials, it puts a strain on our budget. We obtain recently-published adoption books from used bookstores and individuals donate their own gently-used books. Several of our participants earmark monetary donations for our adoption resource library. I also review books on my adoption blog. Authors and publishers send me free review copies, and when I'm finished reviewing them I donate them to the church library or award them as door prizes during our ministry events.

The Heartbeat Ministries shelf in our church library contains about 50 infertility and adoption books—significantly more than you'll find at most brick-and-mortar bookstores. When we promote our books on the church Web site or in the bulletin or newspaper, they fly off the shelves.

WORKSHEET
BUILDING A RESOURCE LIBRARY

List adoption agencies and organizations in your region or state:

Contact them and ask them to recommend their favorite resources:

Ask them to add your ministry to their mailing list and request at least one copy of their information packet, application forms, newsletter, and other promotional materials.

Contact local bookstores and ask whether they provide ministry discounts.

Visit online booksellers such as Amazon, eBay, and Christianbook.com, where you can purchase new or used adoption books at deep discounts.

WORKSHEET
BUILDING A RESOURCE LIBRARY

Visit TapestryBooks.com, the premiere online adoption bookstore. Request to be added to their mailing list to receive news about the latest releases.

Determine how you'll make resource library materials available.

- Does your church have a library?
- If so, is the librarian willing to allot space in which to display resources?
- Will you be allowed to display both Christian and general market (secular) resources?
- Does your library accept new books only, or can you donate gently-used books?
- If your sponsor does not have a library, is there a classroom, a cupboard, or an office in which you can store materials?
- Will your sponsor's governing body permit you to set up a resource table? If so, what types of materials can you display and where/when can you showcase them?

If there is no convenient place to store/distribute materials, you can still make them available. Here are some possibilities:

- E-mail bibliographies of adoption books to your group's participants. Find out who owns certain books and ask whether they're willing to lend them out.
- Create a book distribution system (either by postal mail or in-person) and publicize it via e-mail or your group's Web site.
- Purchase several copies of a book at a discount and use it as an adoption "book club" selection.

WORKSHEET
BUILDING A RESOURCE LIBRARY

⚔ Establish a partnership with your local public library.

- List the adoption books available at the public library.
- Acquaint the librarian with your group and provide the librarian with a list of recommended books (including ISBN numbers) you'd like to see purchased.
- Volunteer to create an adoption book display when the new books arrive.

MENTORING PROGRAM

I was heading out the door after church one Sunday when I spotted a long-time Heartbeat Ministries participant cradling a newborn baby. She beckoned me over, grinning from ear-to-ear.

Unable to contain my excitement, I blurted, "Is this *your* baby?"

"Yes, we adopted him last week. And you were a big part of the whole process," she added.

Because so many people who experience adoption feel isolated, mentoring is a critical component of an adoption support network. In many cases—particularly when there aren't enough participants to form a small group—one-to-one mentoring becomes the sole focus of a support network.

The most effective mentors are people in your church or community who have "lived" adoption. At Heartbeat Ministries, we match people who request a mentor with someone of the same gender who has experienced similar issues.

For example, we pair a woman grieving a failed adoption with another woman who has experienced a failed adoption. We match a couple considering adopting from Korea with a couple who has recently adopted from Korea. We introduce a single woman adopting from foster care to a single woman who has completed a foster-adoption. We acquaint a woman considering placing a child in an open adoption with a woman who has an open adoption with her child.

While a few of our mentors are professional counselors or trained peer counselors, most are lay people who have experienced adoption firsthand. Our ministry doesn't have the financial resources to train mentors, and we explain that fact to all who request mentors. We assure them that while our mentors are not counselors, they are extraordinarily sensitive to the needs of others, by virtue of having experienced adoption themselves.

Mentors and the people they care for mutually agree on the type of relationship they want. Sometimes a few phone calls, e-mails and/or visits suffice. Others form long-term friendships or start a support group together.

WORKSHEET
SETTING UP A MENTORING PROGRAM

A member of your leadership team must screen potential mentors, create suitable matches among mentors and those who have requested them, and monitor the mentoring partnership.

Screening Mentors

Interview adoptive parents, birth parents, adopted persons, or adoption professionals within your network who possess the following qualities:

- Comfortable articulating thoughts and feelings about adoption
- Compassionate towards others
- Committed to listening, supporting, and praying, rather than advising
- Engaged in a growing relationship with Christ

Create a spreadsheet that details contact information about your mentors and their area(s) of expertise. Mentors might include:

- Transracial families
- Parents who adopted healthy Caucasian newborns
- Parents who adopted internationally (organized by country)
- People who adopted after age 40
- Single parents
- Foster parents
- Adult adopted persons
- Birth parents in open or closed adoptions
- Birth parents/adoptees seeking to be reunited
- Parents whose children have experienced attachment issues
- Parents who adopted children with special needs
- Parents who adopted independently/privately

⚑ Parents who experienced pregnancy loss or adoption loss

⚑ Parents who faced fertility challenges

Creating Matches

Interview the person who requests a mentor. Ask:

⚑ Where are you in the adoption process?

⚑ For what specific issues do you desire support?

⚑ What is the estimated time period for which you're requesting support? (Examples: holiday season, Mother's Day, from now until the adoption takes place)

⚑ Do you prefer to meet in person, talk on the phone, send e-mails, or a combination?

⚑ What type of mentor(s) do you prefer?

Monitoring Mentorships

Both parties in the mentorship must establish boundaries on their relationship. They should discuss and agree upon the following prior to their first meeting:

⚑ What will our level of involvement be?

- We will exchange _____ e-mails per week, on average.
- If one person sends an e-mail and doesn't get a response, we will wait _____ days before following up.
- We will meet for coffee _____ (Every other week? Monthly?).
- The best/worst days and times for phone calls are _____.
- We will limit our phone calls to _____ minutes apiece.

- Our mentorship will continue for _____ weeks/months.

The mentoring program coordinator should periodically check in with both parties to ensure regular contact is being made and both parties are satisfied with the relationship. If either party expresses discomfort or dissatisfaction, the coordinator can troubleshoot the situation or assign a new mentor. If the mentee becomes overly dependent on his or her mentor, the program leader should arrange for a different mentor or should advise pastoral or professional counseling.

To prevent mentor burnout, avoid overusing your mentors. Alleviating burnout is a challenge in small communities where few mentors are available. Check in regularly with your mentors, thanking them for the valuable service they provide and encouraging them to take a break from mentoring whenever they need one.

THE ONLINE CONNECTION

The Internet offers a smorgasbord of free and low-cost options to supplement face-to-face adoption ministry. Possibilities include Web sites, blogs, podcasts, conference calls, teleseminars, e-newsletters, e-mail discussion groups, message boards, and chat rooms.

Web site. Your group's Web site will serve as the hub for your online presence. It can stand alone or be embedded within your sponsoring organization's site. Your site can include the following:

- Information about your group and its mission
- Member news
  - Upcoming adoption travel
  - Homecomings
  - Prayer requests
  - Inspiring stories
- Schedule of events
- Adoption information
  - Articles and essays by members
  - Adoption devotionals and Bible studies
  - Adoption news
  - Updates about the ever-changing adoption regulations worldwide
  - Links to public and private agencies, facilitators, and adoption attorneys in your area
  - Links to adoption search and reunion registries
  - Links to adoption organizations and support groups in your area
  - Links to Christian Internet support groups
  - Links to Christian adoption blogs and/or to member adoption blogs and personal adoption Web sites

- Links to cultural festivals, fairs, and events in your area
- Links to adoption photo listings of waiting children
- Links to adoption magazines, books, and other products (create a free Amazon Associates aStore and earn referral fees for all adoption products sold via your store. You can embed your aStore within your Web site or link to it from your site)

Blog. A blog (or Weblog) is a low-cost, easy-to-use, interactive Web site—a social networking tool that builds community among your group's members and expands your ministry worldwide. Your blog can serve as your group's primary online presence or it can be embedded in your group's Web site.

Written by one or several members of your group, a blog communicates information and shares personal reflections and anecdotes. Because the content is always fresh, a blog engages readers on an ongoing basis.

A blog is also a highly effective way to spread the word about your organization and to connect with other adoption support organizations. Best of all, blog hosting companies such as Typepad and Blogger make it easy for non-techies to get a blog up and running within half an hour.

Podcasts. When you teach adoption workshops and seminars, always record them digitally. You can repackage them as podcasts (audio/MP3 or video files) people can download or watch/listen to via your Web site, blog, e-mail, or e-newsletter. Because they engage additional senses, podcasts add personality to your group's online presence.

Conference Calls. If you need to conduct a meeting and face challenges getting everyone together, schedule a conference call. Hosting services (see "Recommended Web Sites" in Appendix) provide you with a dial-in teleconferencing line and allow you to record your call and distribute it via RSS and podcasts.

Teleseminars. Online training sessions, workshops, interviews, radio shows, meetings, and Q & A sessions are called teleseminars. During teleseminars, workshop participants listen to the audio portion of the seminar over their phone as they view the visual portion on their desktop (for hosting services, see "Recommended Web Sites" in Appendix).

E-newsletter. Electronic newsletters and magazines (called e-newsletters and e-zines) offer yet another means of encouraging relationships and publicizing your group. Like their print counterparts, e-newsletters provide information, tips, and resources; they profile group members, announce upcoming events and adoptions, and list prayer requests.

Because people read 25–30 percent slower on a computer screen than they do on paper, limit your e-newsletter to 800 words. Depending on the scope of your network, you can publish your e-newsletter weekly, bi-weekly, monthly, or quarterly.

In addition to e-mailing a plain text version or rich text HTML version to subscribers, you should publish the newsletter on your group's Web site.

Before you publish your first e-newsletter, create a database of interested people and ask them to subscribe. E-newsletters that do not require a subscription process are considered spam (unsolicited commercial e-mail) and can result in Internet service providers blacklisting all e-mails from your address. Every newsletter you e-mail must also contain an "unsubscribe" option; you are ethically obligated to honor all "unsubscribe" requests.

If you're technologically challenged, the most convenient way to publish an e-zine is to subscribe to a service that provides customizable newsletter templates, manages subscriber lists, and sends newsletters (for hosting services, see "Recommended Web Sites" in Appendix).

E-mail discussion group. When your group's members are unable to have "face time," they can remain connected via an interactive e-mail discussion group. At Heartbeat Ministries, we use our e-mail group only for announcing upcoming meetings, for requesting volunteers/mentors, and for posting prayer requests and praise reports. We chose to limit the use of our e-mail group because we don't want to inundate our participants with a constant stream of e-mails.

Here's how e-mail discussion groups work: When a subscriber sends an e-mail to the group's central mailing address, the automated host distributes that e-mail to everyone who subscribes to the group. Most hosts (Yahoo! Groups is the most popular free hosting service) offer a "digest" mode which compiles the entire day's messages into one e-mail. Subscribers can opt not to receive e-mail, but to read the messages at the group's Home page, instead.

You can test-drive Yahoo! Groups by creating one for your leadership team or by creating a group to be used solely for prayer requests. As your adoption network grows, you can expand your topic or add additional groups for birth parents, waiting parents, parents of toddlers, or families adopting internationally.

Message board/bulletin board. Message boards (also called "discussion forums") provide your participants with a Web-based arena in which to ask questions, share information, and express opinions. Your leadership team can also use electronic bulletin boards to post an event calendar and to poll your group's members (for bulletin board services, see "Recommended Web Sites" in Appendix).

Chat room. Your group's participants can interact live via their keyboards in a private chat room. Inexpensive software lets you create a customizable chat room that runs directly from your Web site. To begin chatting, users simply type in a screen name of their choice and a password (for chat room software, see "Recommended Web Sites" in Appendix).

WORKSHEET
ESTABLISHING ON ONLINE PRESENCE

Check the online features that seem most appropriate for your adoption support network:

- ☐ Web site
- ☐ Blog
- ☐ Podcasts
- ☐ Conference Calls
- ☐ Teleseminars
- ☐ E-newsletter
- ☐ E-mail discussion group
- ☐ Message board
- ☐ Chat room

List Web sites of companies that host the online features you've selected.

Create a comparison chart that details each company's features, ease of use, training, customer support, and fee structure.

SOCIAL EVENTS

Your group's social activities can encompass anything that captures your imagination. Adoptive families from within your network can get together for kid-friendly outings that include barbeques, picnics, or potlucks. Families enjoy activities that celebrate their child's ethnic and cultural heritage. Many communities and adoption agencies host cultural festivals or heritage camps throughout the year. Consider attending a cultural event as a group. If you're really ambitious, your group can host its own cultural event.

Your group can host a "family fun night" for your church. The evening can include arts and crafts, giant inflatable toys, carnival games, a musical or dramatic presentation, and a guest speaker who shares about adoption. In conjunction with family fun night, your group can plan a charitable activity such as an orphanage fund-raiser, a school supply drive, or a winter coat drive for foster children.

Social activities work well within the structure of small groups and support groups. For instance, a support group for waiting moms can meet monthly at a restaurant. After the members adopt, the group can morph into a "new moms" or "moms of toddlers" group and can continue to meet—at parks with playgrounds, of course.

Social events also spawn small groups. If you launch a support group and it flops, consider sticking with social events for a while. Once members of the larger group get acquainted, they may decide to form a support group or to mentor one another individually.

Potential social events include:

- Camping trips
- Museum visits
- Swimming at the pool, lakefront, or beach

- Hosting a booth at the county fair/community festival
- Dessert evening combined with a roundtable discussion
- Bowling
- Women's-only or men's-only outings
- Movie/video night
- Ice cream social
- Karaoke night
- Scrapbooking social
- Skating party
- Entering a walk-a-thon or bike-a-thon together
- Day-long or overnight retreat

BABY ITEM EXCHANGE

A typical pregnancy lasts nine months. But for foster or adoptive parents, "pregnancy" might span only a few hours:

Foster children appear on their foster parents' doorsteps in the blink of an eye.

Parents waiting to adopt internationally receive long-awaited travel authorizations and hop on the next flight to China.

Parents adopting newborns are surprised by a phone call from their case worker, who announces, "A woman who just gave birth decided to place her baby for adoption. She picked you. Get to the hospital. *Now.*"

A baby item exchange serves families who learn at the last minute that their child will be coming home—families who don't possess all the accoutrements needed to begin raising a baby.

Your entire faith community can participate in a baby item exchange. The program's coordinator creates a spreadsheet that lists contact information for people willing to loan or give away cribs, car seats, high chairs, playpens, or strollers. Donors store the items at their homes (unless a participant or your hosting

organization volunteers to provide storage space). When some-one requests to borrow an item, the coordinator schedules the delivery. A baby item exchange is a simple, practical way for the community at-large to participate in adoption support.

WORKSHOPS

Nothing impacts a person contemplating adoption more than hearing about it from someone who's "been there, done that." The most popular component of Heartbeat Ministries is our "Exploring Adoption" workshops—a five-week series we host at our church every other year. During each session, guest panelists—adoptive parents, birth parents, adoption social workers, and adoption attorneys—share information and life stories about various aspects of adoption. We encourage inter-action among the panelists and audience and allot a significant portion of each session for questions.

Guest speakers. If you live in a metropolitan area and have access to adoption professionals, they are almost always willing to speak at workshops. While you can expect them to mention their agency/service, adoption professionals understand that their purpose is to acquaint people with adoption rather than make a sales pitch.

The non-partisan setting gives those considering adoption the opportunity to interact with adoption professionals. Often, attendees engage the services of a particular adoption service provider based on the connection they make with the person during the workshop.

While it's important to include one or two adoption pro-fessionals among your panelists, your most compelling speak-ers will be adoptive parents and birth parents. During one of our "Exploring Adoption" workshops, my husband and I and our sons' birth parents discussed open adoption. Several years later, I ran into a woman who had attended that workshop. She asked me how our sons' birth parents were doing, calling them each by name.

My mouth dropped open. "How did you remember their names?"

"Your talk made such a huge impression on my husband and me that I will never forget their names," she replied. "Because of that talk we decided to pursue open adoption."

That couple, who adopted twins, have a fantastic relationship with their daughters' birth mother and her family. They and their daughters' birth mother now share their own experiences with open adoption during "Exploring Adoption" workshops.

When birth parents and adoptive parents volunteer to speak at adoption workshops, they feel compelled to acquaint people with adoption's challenges as well as its joys. They tell it like it is. And that's just what people who are feeling insecure and uncertain about adoption want and need.

After attending the workshops, some participants decide not to pursue adoption. Others choose a different method of adoption than they'd originally intended. No matter what their choice, they inevitably comment that the information helped them make an informed choice.

Resource Materials. In addition to inviting guest speakers to share their experiences with adoption, set up a resource table that contains information packets from adoption agencies, facilitators, and attorneys in your area. Stock your table with a selection of current adoption books, magazines, and articles. You will have to do some legwork to obtain these materials, but those who attend your meetings will hungrily pounce on any resources you provide (see the Appendix for recommended resources and workshop curriculum materials).

Partnering. Partnering is particularly effective in small communities where it's difficult to recruit enough workshop leaders and participants. Consider joining forces with local churches and adoption organizations. They'll help organize workshops and will invite their members. Partnering gives you access to a wider variety of guest speakers and the ability to reach more people interested in adoption.

Number of sessions. At Heartbeat Ministries, we've tried everything from nine-week sessions to five-week sessions. We've hosted quarterly and once-a-month workshops, but the time lag between those workshops failed to create continuity among attendees. We discovered that five consecutive weeks is an appropriate amount of time in which to touch on vital adoption issues and to hold people's interest and attendance.

Registration and fees. It's difficult to predict how many people will attend workshops. We have had anywhere from five to 35 attendees, depending on the topic. Once, we invited six guest speakers and only three people attended the workshop. It was awkward, especially for the red-faced facilitator who felt guilty about wasting the guest speakers' time.

While such scenarios are common, you can work them to your advantage, pulling the chairs into an intimate circle and having an informal discussion. The guest panelists rarely mind switching gears, especially if you warn them in advance that attendance might be minimal.

Requiring pre-registration (or at least encouraging it) gives you a better idea of how many people to expect at each session. You should contact registrants before each meeting to confirm their attendance and to promote the topic-of-the-week.

You may need to charge a workshop fee to pay for facility rental or speaker honorariums/gifts. Whenever possible, offer free workshops (a rarity these days) and invite the public. At least half the participants at Heartbeat's "Exploring Adoption" workshops do not attend our church. While we don't evangelize at our meetings, our workshops are faith-based. We open with prayer and close each session by giving people the opportunity to pray for one another.

Facilitators. A facilitator from your leadership team must attend each workshop to ensure a sense of continuity. The facilitator's role is particularly important when attendees aren't acquainted with one another. The facilitator greets attendees and helps them feel comfortable, makes announcements, introduces the guest speakers, asks pertinent questions, and monitors the discussion. If possible, the same person should facilitate the entire workshop series.

The workshop facilitator has a rewarding job. During the years I've facilitated "Exploring Adoption" workshops, I've watched people learn and grow. Often, attendees who begin our workshops knowing next to nothing about adoption go on to adopt children and later volunteer to lead workshops or launch their own support groups. None of us claim to "know it all." We just want to give back—to make the adoption experience a little easier for the next person who travels that road.

Door prizes. Awarding door prizes is a fun way to promote your workshops and to generate enthusiasm among attendees. When we plan our "Exploring Adoption" workshops, we contact authors/publishers of adoption books and ask them to donate books we can award as door prizes. We've given away novels with adoption themes as well as children's books, adoption memoirs, adoption anthologies, and "how to adopt" manuals. It's a great way to introduce prospective parents to adoption literature.

If your budget allows, you can purchase gift subscriptions for magazines such as *Adoptive Families, Adoption TODAY, or Fostering Families TODAY* and give them as door prizes.

Encourage participants in your network to donate their own door prizes, as well. One member of our group donated items she'd purchased in China during her adoption trip. Another family donated an adoption agency calendar that featured their child on the cover. Local adoption agencies donated bookmarks, mouse pads, mugs, pens, magnets, and other giveaway items.

The Adoption Network

WORKSHOP TOPICS

Need a topic for an adoption workshop? Here are some popular ones for adoptive parents:

- Myths and fears about adoption
- Moving from infertility to adoption
- The adoption home study
  - Guest speaker: Adoption professional
- International adoption
  - Panelists: Parents who have adopted from different countries
- Domestic open adoption
  - Panelists: Birth parents, adoptive parents, and older adopted children
- Creative adoption financing
  - Guest speaker: Financial Advisor
- Single parent adoption
- Surviving a disrupted or failed adoption
- Adopting after age 40
- Biblical foundations for adoption
- Internet resources for adoption
- Agency versus independent adoption
- Creating an adoptive family profile
- Legal aspects of adoption
  - Guest speaker: Adoption attorney
- Adopting sibling groups
- Adopted and biological siblings
- Transracial adoption
- Transcultural adoption
- Preparing for foster parenting
- Foster-to-adopt
- Older child adoption
- Special needs adoption

- ✍ Breastfeeding the adopted baby
- ✍ Parenting your newborn
- ✍ Issues adoptive families face
- ✍ Confronting adoption prejudice
- ✍ Developmental stages in adopted children
  - Guest speaker: Child development specialist
- ✍ Adoption medicine
  - Guest speaker: Pediatrician specializing in adoption medicine
- ✍ Adult adopted person's perspective on adoption
- ✍ Educating friends and relatives about adoption
- ✍ Supporting families who are waiting to adopt

SUPPORT GROUPS

While the adoption of our first child progressed smoothly and exceptionally quickly, our second adoption frazzled our emotions. During the year we waited for our son, four almost-adoptions failed to materialize, leaving us glassy-eyed with grief. How I wish we'd joined a support group to help us through that difficult time!

While many secular adoption support groups exist, few are faith-based. Since faith issues regularly surface during the adoption process, a Christian support group benefits its members in ways a secular group can't: members mutually seek God's guidance, wisdom, and comfort and they uphold one another through prayer. Members also share information and resources.

Within your adoption network, support groups may spring up for infertile couples, for people waiting to adopt, for parents who have recently adopted, for adult adopted people, or for birth/first parents. Support groups must be needs-based; don't start a group with only a vague notion someone might show up. Wait until several people express an interest and commit to attending. That way, you'll have the critical mass needed to form an effective group.

Launching your group

First, define the goals you want the group to accomplish and set an ending date for the group. Support groups are short-term commitments, usually lasting six weeks, ten weeks, three months, or six months. At the end of your group's cycle, members will evaluate whether the group's goals were accomplished. They will decide whether to:

- disband
- continue as usual
- invite new members
- re-form as a new group
- change the group's focus

Establishing an ending date frees everyone to move on from the group without guilt.

Learn whether similar groups exist. Collect information about other groups by contacting area churches, family therapists, libraries, social service agencies, and adoption organizations. Consult the classified ads in your local newspapers and parenting magazines for information, as well. Consider joining or networking with these groups, or launching a local chapter of an existing nationwide or regional group.

Select a facilitator. Every support group needs a facilitator to monitor the clock, ensure everyone receives an equal opportunity to share, and steer participants back on track when they "bird walk." The facilitator can be a member of the support group or can be someone such as a pastor, ministry coordinator, counselor, or a member of your adoption network's leadership team.

Name your group. Some people shy away from the term "support group," assuming it implies emotional instability. Consider alternative names such as the following:

- ✍ Discussion Forum
- ✍ Resource Group
- ✍ Adoption Connection
- ✍ _____ Adoptive Families Association
- ✍ Parent Network
- ✍ Family Forum
- ✍ Adoptive Families of _____
- ✍ Acronyms such as WISH (Waiting Is So Hard) or SNAP (Society of Special Needs Adoptive Parents)

Arrange for a meeting location. While churches, community centers, and other public facilities are good places to meet, they don't offer the warmth, anonymity, and intimacy of a private home.

If you meet in a public facility, you'll need to book a room and appoint people to set up tables and chairs, media equipment, and refreshments and to clean up after each meeting.

Post a discreet sign that points the way to your meeting room. Many attendees feel reticent or embarrassed to join a support group. Nothing scares them off faster than a sign with big red letters that shouts, "SUPPORT GROUP MEETS HERE."

If you meet in a home, decide whether to meet in the same home every time or to rotate among homes. Determine the host's responsibilities, taking care not to overburden the host.

Decide whether to offer childcare. If so, you'll need to screen and hire caregivers, plan activities, arrange for a place for the children to meet, and budget funds to pay childcare providers. (Note: for safety and liability reasons, have two childcare workers with the children at all times.)

Decide whether to charge fees. If your group rents a facility or pays childcare providers, you may need to charge membership fees. Determine exactly what the fees will be used for and note when they'll be collected (one-time only, periodically, or at each meeting).

Decide whether to invite women only, men only, or couples. When Heartbeat Ministries launched an infertility support group, we invited couples. We opened the group to the public, and couples from several churches joined. One of our member couples attended a church in which assisted reproductive technology was frowned upon. The couple didn't feel safe at their own church sharing the fact that they were receiving medical treatment for infertility, and they valued the nonjudgmental fellowship among the Christians in our group.

During our support group's first few meetings several of the men were reluctant to speak, but as time went on they began sharing openly. The participants decided to be a "closed" group; once the core group was established, they did not invite new members. The couples formed a strong bond, and met once a month for a year and a half.

Issue personal invitations. While a classified ad in your local newspaper or a notice on the supermarket bulletin board might draw some attendees, people are most receptive to personal invitations. Issue them face-to-face, over the phone, or via e-mail. When people believe their presence is desired and valued, they're more likely to attend.

If you invite people from other churches, send a brochure or letter that introduces your group and its sponsoring organization. Include a sample bulletin/newsletter announcement and encourage the pastor to broadcast your group to his or her congregation.

Create a visitor's policy.

- ✍ Will you welcome visitors to your group?
- ✍ Must group members be informed before a visitor attends?
- ✍ How many visitors may attend each meeting?
- ✍ How many times can the same visitor attend?
- ✍ Can visitors become members?
- ✍ Can visitors participate during the sharing portion of the meeting, or are they silent observers?

Decide how to support one another between meetings. If your group meets once a month, members will likely want to interact on a more regular basis. They can do so via a blog, e-mail discussion group, online bulletin board, chat room, on the phone, or in person. Set boundaries around acceptable and unacceptable interaction practices. A group can die quickly if one member learns that other members have been gossiping about him or her outside of meetings.

Structuring meetings

Support group meetings usually last about two hours and begin with socializing (refreshments are a must). Limit social time to 10–15 minutes; it can eat up your entire meeting. Another alternative is to schedule social time at the end of meetings. After people have spent an hour or two together, they're usually more revved up to share ideas and begin building friendships.

Give each attendee the opportunity to provide an update and to share experiences and feelings. Topics that emerge during updates will result in lively discussions. Depending on the size of your group, you may need to limit updates to 5–10 minutes apiece.

After the updates, the group can discuss a particular topic or study a book or Bible passage. Periodically invite guest speakers to meetings; their fresh perspective will inject new life into discussions. Sometime during your meeting, share prayer requests and ways in which God has responded to prayers. Then pray for one another (make sure people understand they have the option to pray out loud or to listen).

Discussion topics. Adoption support groups discuss a wide range of topics. You can invite a guest speaker to share expertise on a particular topic; you can discuss an adoption-themed book, or you can ask group members to facilitate discussions about topics that interest them. Here are some suggested topics for an adoptive parent support group:

- Adoption Medicine Specialists
- Adoption Travel
- Agreeing With Your Spouse to Adopt
- Attachment and Bonding
- Biblical Foundations of Adoption
- Creating a Lifebook for Your Child
- Creative Adoption Financing
- Cultural Opportunities for Adoptive Families
- Discussing Adoption with Your Child's Teacher/Class
- Establishing Relationships with Birth Parents
- Federal Adoption Tax Credit
- Grieving Adoption Loss
- Helpful Adoption Web Sites and Blogs
- Hosting Programs for Orphans
- Institutionalized Children
- Language Acquisition
- Meeting the Birth Family
- Myths About Adoption
- Older Child Adoption
- Pre- and Post-Adoption Paperwork
- Post-Adoption Depression
- Raising Adopted Children

- ⚞ Responding to Insensitive Comments
- ⚞ Special Needs Sunday School
- ⚞ Transitioning from Fostering to Adoption
- ⚞ Transracial Adoption Issues
- ⚞ Working with Your Adoption Professional

Creating a covenant

A covenant is the container that holds your group; written guidelines that encompass who you are and where you want to go. Well-written guidelines reduce anxiety, angry outbursts, and hurt feelings among group members.

Two common complaints among support groups are that certain members monopolize sharing time and/or offer unsolicited advice. A well-written covenant addresses these issues and minimizes the chances of them occurring. When problems arise, the group's facilitator should review the covenant with the entire group or privately, with the offender.

When our infertility support group formed, our guidelines stated that everything said during our meetings would remain confidential. We also agreed to avoid clinic or doctor bashing/praising, with the understanding that two people may have entirely different experiences with the same practitioner.

WORKSHEET
CREATING SUPPORT GROUP GUIDELINES

Name of Group:

Our Purpose:

> *Example:* To provide a warm Christian fellowship where we can learn about adoption, discuss adoption-related issues, affirm one another's decision to adopt, and encourage each other through conversation and prayer.

Desired Results:

> *Example:* To help people feel confident and at peace with their decision about whether to pursue adoption.

To decrease the sense of isolation pre-adoptive families feel.

Meeting Location:

WORKSHEET
CREATING SUPPORT GROUP GUIDELINES

Length of Meetings:

Frequency of Meetings:
Example: Weekly for nine weeks, with the option to re-structure at the conclusion of nine weeks.

When Members are Added:

Meeting Format:

Covenant:
Example: Every member must agree upon and sign the covenant. Portions of the following covenant are adapted from The Quaker Model of Careful Listening.

☐ We will start and end meetings on time.
☐ We will make every effort to attend meetings during the group's _____ week duration.
☐ We will call the facilitator if we can't make it to a meeting. If we choose to leave the group, we will communicate that decision to the facilitator.

WORKSHEET
CREATING SUPPORT GROUP GUIDELINES

- ☐ We agree that every person is an expert on his or her own experience. We will speak of our own experiences, wants, needs, desires, and feelings. We will avoid rescuing, problem-solving, debating, offering advice, or feeling responsible for alleviating someone else's pain.
- ☐ We understand that our most important contribution to the group is grateful listening. We will allow each person to finish his or her story without interrupting. As we listen empathetically, we will use nonverbal cues to communicate caring and concern.
- ☐ We will give everyone who wishes to share the opportunity. We will not pressure anyone to share; we will allow silence to speak to us.
- ☐ We understand that the experiences others share often illuminate insights into our own experiences. After everyone has had a chance to talk, we may share again, time permitting.
- ☐ We will be sensitive, affirming, and loving.
- ☐ We will stay on topic. The facilitator will guide us back if we stray off topic.
- ☐ We will make every attempt to read suggested materials in preparation for the following meeting.
- ☐ We will maintain confidentiality. We will not discuss anything shared during our meetings outside the group else unless given explicit permission.
- ☐ We will respect group members' decision to pursue options other than adoption. For those who choose adoption, we will respect differences regarding the type of adoption intended (independent, agency, domestic, foster-adopt, international, etc.).
- ☐ We will pray for each other, both at group meetings and during personal prayer time throughout the week.

PRAYER MINISTRY

In his letter to the Ephesians, the apostle Paul encourages us to "pray on all occasions with all kinds of prayers and requests" and to "be strong in the Lord and in his mighty power."[13] Prayer is the vital component of any adoption support network. As you pray with joyful expectation, God will surprise you by unfolding your ministry in ways you never imagined.

Your church probably has a prayer team or individuals committed to praying for those involved in church leadership. Contact them and ask them to pray for your adoption ministry's leaders and mission.

Not only does your support network itself need to be regularly uplifted in prayer, but your group's participants crave prayers on their behalf:

- People pondering adoption (both prospective adoptive parents and pregnant women) need prayer to guide their decision-making.
- People who released a child for adoption need prayer to help them work through their grief.
- People waiting to adopt need prayer for peace and for God's will to be done.
- Parents embarking on overseas travel need prayer for a safe journey and for smooth adoption proceedings.
- Foster-to-adopt parents need prayer before, during, and after volatile court hearings.
- Those who were unable to adopt a hoped-for child need prayer for healing.

Prayer is simply a matter of talking with God; there are myriad ways for that to happen within the context of your support network:

- Create an Internet prayer chain, e-mailing requests or posting them to your group's electronic bulletin board, blog, e-newsletter, or discussion group.
- Form a team of people who commit to pray specifically for your ministry's needs and its participants on an on-going basis. Schedule monthly or quarterly dates when prayer team members will be available to pray with individual participants before or after a church service.
- Establish prayer partnerships with area churches who are invested in adoption support.
- Alert your church staff that Mother's Day and Father's Day are the most difficult Sundays of the year for those who are grieving the loss of a child and for those who yearn for a child. Request a special prayer on behalf of grieving and waiting parents, or volunteer to write a prayer and share it during your church service. Many churches celebrate Mother's and Father's Day by asking parents to stand and be recognized or by giving them a flower. These types of celebrations are emotional minefields for:
  - Infertile people
  - Those grieving pregnancy loss or a failed adoption
  - Those who have relinquished a child for adoption
  - Those waiting to become parents through birth or adoption

Suggest that your church plan low-key Mother's/Father's Day celebrations and ask church leaders to recognize all those who play a loving role in a child's life.

- Plan a prayer service for those who are waiting for a child. Incorporate it into a regular church service or host a special event.

TRAINING CHURCH LEADERS

I vividly remember the time I contacted the editor of a magazine for church leaders and proposed writing an article instructing pastors how to support adoptive families-in-waiting.

The editor sent the following terse reply: "Your idea doesn't suggest anything most of our readers couldn't figure out for themselves. And the insensitive ones who would need such a piece probably don't read our magazine."

That editor was dead wrong, as the conversations I've had with adoptive parents attest. Here's a sampling of how some pastors "support" those who long to create families:

> "We asked our pastor if we could start a support group for families waiting to adopt. He responded, 'We don't need that type of group. So many people in our church are dying and getting divorced. Your issue is minor in comparison to theirs.'"

> "My pastor preached that infertile women are barren because of their attitude. He said, 'Bad attitudes cause a chemical imbalance that keeps us from reproducing.'"

> "After waiting years for a child, I felt discouraged and lonely. A woman from our women's ministry team told me my feelings of loneliness were a result of believing 'a lie from the pit of hell.' She then informed me that once I adopt, I'll get pregnant.

> My pastor's wife, observing my tears, grabbed my arm and told me God wanted her to pray for my 'womb to open' because God must have closed it for some reason. She says I should put my discouragement in God's hands and not worry about it. She even deletes my prayer requests from the weekly prayer chain."

"We had been waiting several years to adopt when a friend from church cheerfully informed us, 'Look on the bright side. The fact that there are no babies to adopt means there are fewer promiscuous teenagers.'"

"The first time my husband and I told our pastor about our fertility challenges, our pastor said with an awkward smile, 'Well, why don't you just try the Petri dish?' We could tell he was feeling uncomfortable discussing this with us, so we ended the conversation. He's never mentioned 'our situation' again."

"I started an orphan ministry at my church and I asked my pastor if he would do a sermon about adoption. He replied, 'I don't think adoption is worth doing a sermon about.'"

When you launch your adoption support network, you'll have your work cut out for you if your church leaders are inflicted with the same Foot-In-Mouth disease as those in the examples. People who are uninformed about adoption overcompensate by speaking without thinking, by saying too much, or by saying nothing at all. You must teach them:

- How adoption works in the 21st century (See Appendix for recommended resources)
- How to use respectful adoption language
- How to respond appropriately to adoption-related questions

If your pastor seems resistant to adoption, find out why. Schedule a private meeting with your pastor and have a frank discussion. Explain your interest in adoption and acquaint your pastor with hurtful comments that have been directed your way. Enlist your pastor's help in brainstorming ways to introduce other church leaders to adoption and adoption ministry.

Many churches have lay ministry groups that provide one-to-one care for those who are hurting or facing life changes. These groups are ideal venues for you to educate church leaders about adoption. With your pastor's blessing, contact the caregiving ministry's coordinator and volunteer to teach a workshop about adoption support at one of their training sessions.

You can also train those in your church who work with children, providing them with resources and tips that will help them understand the issues adopted children face. Because church leaders are incredibly busy, it's wise to incorporate your training sessions into one of their regularly-scheduled meetings.

When you train peer counselors, actively involve them, role-playing the following scenarios:

> You are a lay minister and have begun meeting with a woman who is waiting to adopt a child. She is angry because people constantly tell her, "If you adopt you'll get pregnant." How will you help the woman respond appropriately to this unsolicited advice?

> The parents of a teenage girl from your congregation confide they've just learned their daughter is pregnant. They tell you, "She wants to raise her baby herself, but we want her to place it for adoption." How will you help the family work through this crisis?

> You know a couple who has been waiting several years to adopt. They tell you they feel discouraged and wonder whether God is punishing them. How will you respond?

> A grieving couple who had to return the baby they'd hoped to adopt to his birth parents come to you, distraught. What comforting words will you offer?

A woman who recently released her child for adoption visits you. She confides, "At first I thought I'd made the right decision, but now I'm not so sure." How will you respond?

A man who is going through the adoption process tells you, "I have always been in control of my life. But the adoption process makes me feel totally out of control." How will you respond?

During your training session, introduce caregivers to several inappropriate and appropriate responses to typical adoption-related concerns.

Inappropriate Responses

- *You shouldn't feel so unhappy* (minimizes the person's feelings and makes him or her feel even more sad—and guilty for feeling sad).
- *Have you tried praying about it?* (sounds condescending and accusing; assumes praying about it will automatically solve the problem).
- *God must be trying to teach you a lesson. He will bless you with a child when you are completely in His will* (assumes the person is a hopeless case and puts the caregiver in the role of playing "God").

Appropriate Responses

- *I don't know much about adoption, but I'd like to learn. Would you share your story with me?* (open-ended and non-judgmental; shows a willingness to learn).
- *I understand that waiting to adopt/placing a child for adoption is one of the most stressful events that can happen to a person* (encourages deeper sharing).
- *My heart aches for you* (demonstrates empathy).

⚔ *In what specific ways are you feeling out of control? What are some things you could do to regain some of the control you feel you've lost?* (pinpoints the underlying issue and introduces problem-solving).

⚔ *May I pray with or for you?* (helps the person feel as you're in this together).

⚔ *May I have permission to pray publicly on your behalf? If so, how can I state the prayer so it is encouraging to you?* (assures the person his or her concern is valid).

⚔ *I don't believe God wants to see you hurting. May I share encouraging Scripture verses with you?* (gives the person hope).

The most important reminder you can give church leaders is that attentive listening speaks louder than words. Warm hugs speak the loudest of all.

As you train church leaders for adoption ministry, acquaint them with respectful adoption terminology. Here are a few examples:

⚔ Use "was adopted" rather than "is adopted." The word "adopted" does not label a person's identity; it describes a legal action that took place.

⚔ When introducing an adoptive family, say, "This is so and so's daughter/son" rather than "This is so and so's *adopted* daughter/son. Calling attention to the manner in which a child entered his or her family makes a child feel strange and unusual.

⚔ Use "first parent" or "birth parent" rather than "real parent" or "natural parent." Note: Some birth parents prefer to be called "natural parents," believing the term "birth parent" is condescending and derogatory. Adoptive parents, on the other hand, balk at the term "natural parent," believing its use relegates them to the role of "unnatural parent." In reality, both birth parents *and* adoptive parents are a child's "real" parents—the child's first parent(s) cared for him or her in the womb, and the adoptive parents raise the child. The term "birth parent" or "first parent" is used mainly to prevent confusion during conversations in which both birth and adoptive parents are included.

- Use "placed a child for adoption," "made an adoption plan," or "chose adoption" rather than "gave up for adoption" or "put up for adoption."
- Use "chose to parent" rather than "kept the baby."
- Use "intercountry adoption" or "international adoption" rather than "foreign adoption."
- Use "out-of-home placement" or "foster care placement" rather than "unwanted child."

It's important for church leaders to understand the needs of adoptive families; leaders must also learn to care for those in their congregation who experience an unplanned pregnancy. Women in crisis pregnancies often turn first to their pastor (or to a pastor of another local church) for counsel and resources. Prepare your pastor by taking him or her on a field trip to local agencies and by supplying your pastor with current resources from the following organizations:

- Maternity homes
- Pro-life pregnancy resource centers
- Christian adoption agencies
- Adoption facilitators and attorneys
- State-run adoption agency (obtain a copy of your state's adoption laws and review it with your pastor)
- Battered women's shelters
- Homeless shelters
- Contact information for people in the church or community who have placed a child for adoption

Equipping church leaders for adoption ministry helps them reach out more effectively to those who need support. Not only that, but church leaders who get excited about adoption ministry will exert their considerable influence to generate enthusiasm among others within the faith community.

EDUCATING THE FAITH COMMUNITY

As the spark for adoption ministry ignites among church leaders, you'll begin fanning the flame in the larger faith community. Once members of your congregation catch your vision, they too will become invested in adoption ministry.

You can raise awareness through hosting an "Adoption Sunday."[14] Suggested dates include:

- A Sunday in November (National Adoption Month)
- The Sunday after National Adoption Day (celebrated the Saturday before Thanksgiving)
- A Sunday in May (National Foster Care Month)
- Mother's Day or Father's Day

During Adoption Sunday, birth parents, adoptive families, and adopted children can share testimonies about adoption. The pastor can preach an adoption-themed sermon; songs can focus on God adopting us into His family; people waiting to adopt can be prayed for, and a portion of the offering can be donated to adoption causes.

Orphan and Waiting Child Ministries

Many churches establish orphan ministries, sometimes called "waiting child ministries." Your faith community can participate in the following hands-on activities on behalf of orphaned children:

"Adopt" an orphanage and provide it with ongoing financial aid.

Send short-term mission teams to assist with childcare, medical care, teaching, building projects, and praying on behalf of the children and their caregivers. If your church doesn't have the resources to organize short-term mission teams, consider joining a "voluntourism" trip hosted by a non-profit organization. Voluntourism combines voluntary service in an orphanage with immersion in the native culture (see Appendix for a list of organizations that sponsor humanitarian missions).

Host a supply drive. Collect shoes, blankets, developmental toys, eyeglasses, school supplies, medical supplies and equipment, or other necessities the orphanage requests. Ship the collected items to the orphanage via members of mission teams who visit.

Participate in a hosting program. Organized by adoption agencies and humanitarian organizations, hosting programs bring older children from orphanages in other countries (usually, former Soviet bloc countries) to the United States for a two- to four-week cultural exchange. The children stay with families who are considering adopting them, giving the orphans and prospective families the chance to get to know one another. A high percentage of the children who participate in hosting programs get adopted, either by their host families or by other families they meet during their trip.

Care for children in institutions. In addition to "adopting" orphanages, your faith community can actively love children who live in group homes (homes for youth in crisis). Volunteer to help with maintenance, gardening, carpentry, plumbing, office work, recreational outings, educational tutoring, mental health care, Bible studies, spiritual guidance, providing rides to church and youth group, or serving as house parents.

Provide respite care for foster families.

FamilyLife's Hope For Orphans Ministry offers the following terrific tips for caring for waiting children:

Pray regularly for a waiting child. Visit a waiting child Web site such as rainbowkids.com or adoptUSkids.org and print out a photo and description of a waiting child. Tape it to your dashboard. Every time you get stuck in traffic or are waiting at a stoplight or drive-thru, pray for the child.

Advocate for a waiting child. Tuck a photo of a waiting child in your wallet. When you visit with others, ask if they or someone they know would consider giving the child a home.

Volunteer to become a Court Appointed Special Advocate (CASA), also known as a volunteer guardian ad litem. CASA volunteers are trained to act as first-hand experts on the individual needs of abused and neglected children in foster care. They often speak on behalf of their assigned child in the courtroom.

"Adopt" a local child welfare social worker. Pray for them, take them to an occasional lunch, and send gifts or notes of encouragement.[15]

Women in Crisis Pregnancies

The faith community also has a responsibility to support women in crisis pregnancies:

Volunteer at a local pregnancy resource center, presenting the adoption option to the center's staff and clients.

Befriend women in crisis pregnancy. Offer to drive them to doctor's appointments, pregnancy counseling appointments, job interviews, or school. Do not pressure them to consider adoption; simply be there for them and offer to pray with and for them.

Provide for the needs of women in unplanned pregnancies. Local maternity homes are usually stretched to the limit; members of your faith community can help by providing short-term housing in private homes. Others in the congregation can support the host families by donating food, clothing, and supplies.

Support local maternity homes. Pray for the women and the staff and financially support the home. Provide maternity clothes, teach parenting classes, host showers for the women who decide to parent, and mentor those who are considering adoption.

Create a pregnancy resource center. Many women don't consider adoption because they don't realize adoption offers them the opportunity to remain in contact with their child. Prepare information sheets that describe the varying degrees of openness in adoption. List contact information for local birth families and adoptive families who are willing to share their experiences with open adoption. Provide contact information for recommended pregnancy counselors, adoption agencies/facilitators, adoption social workers, and adoption attorneys.

Adopted People

Your church can support adopted people of all ages. Here are a few suggestions:

Learn about transracial families. If your church population is mostly Caucasian, adopted children of different ethnicities stand out. Some people overcompensate for their discomfort with transracial families by remarking how "special" or "cute" or "different" the children look.

Sometimes, latent prejudices among members of the congregation emerge when transracial families begin attending. If you notice this happening, address it immediately. Ask your pastor to preach on the theme of prejudice and to incorporate suggestions for how to interact with transracial adoptive families.

Learn about medical and behavioral challenges. Many adopted children, particularly those adopted at older ages, have medical or behavioral challenges. Accommodate children with medical challenges and welcome families whose children have severe behavioral challenges, understanding that the problems stem from past traumas the child has experienced. Caregivers and Sunday school teachers should attend workshops to learn how to work with children who have special needs.

Because parents are embarrassed when their child acts out, they often skip the worship service altogether, opting to stay home or to supervise their child in the childcare area. Members of your congregation can take turns caring for the child during the service so his or her parents can attend worship. Parents of medically or behaviorally-challenged children greatly appreciate this form of respite care, as well as offers to babysit so they can go on a date, get some exercise, or have "alone" time.

Add children's books about adoption to your church library. Adoption-themed children's books help adopted and non-adopted children alike understand adoption.

Befriend an adopted child. All children need non-exploitive adults in their lives. Prior to their adoption, some children have never met an adult who simply loves them and roots them on. You can be that person.

Offer adoption search and reunion resources. Many adult adopted people desire to connect with their birth families. Provide contact information for free and low-cost adoption search registries. Offer to serve as intermediary for people who locate their birth families.

Adoptive Parents

Your faith community should also become actively involved in supporting adoptive parents.

Establish an adoption assistance fund to help families overcome the financial obstacles to adoption. Your church can budget seed money, take a special offering for the fund, and/or designate a portion of fund-raising money for adoption assistance.

Potential fund-raisers include:

- Adoption conference with guest experts, keynote speakers, workshops, and adoption agency/facilitator displays
- Auction (CafePress.com helps you create a variety of customized items)
- Banquet
- Benefit concert, performance, or play
- Widget campaign. A widget or "charity badge" is a graphical element embedded in a Web site or blog. You customize your charity badge's text, explaining the cause for which you're soliciting funds. Readers simply click a button to electronically donate funds (see information about *Network For Good* in the Appendix).

Organizations such as Life International (lifeintl.org) help churches allocate funds from the missions budget, benevolence fund, or raised funds toward interest-free loans and/or matching grants for adoption. Life International administers your adoption fund (at no cost to your church or the fund).

Shaohannah's Hope (shaohannahshope.org), a foundation that helps Christian families reduce the financial barrier to adoption, offers a wealth of information for creating an adoption assistance fund. Their free downloadable booklet, "Your Guide to Starting an Adoption Fund," walks you through structuring your fund as either a line item in the church's budget or as an independent, non-profit 501 (c)(3) corporation. The booklet provides links to IRS resources, tips for creating grant guidelines, and ideas for growing your fund.

In her book *Adoption As A Ministry, Adoption As a Blessing,* Michelle Gardner suggests that individual church members offer no-interest or low-interest adoption loans, with an agreement that the loan be repaid when the family receives their federal adoption tax credit.

Offer childcare during adoption travel. Many parents who travel overseas to adopt leave other children home during the trip. Church members can volunteer to provide childcare, meals, house-sitting, or pet-sitting.

Provide meals for new parents. When families adopt or begin caring for a new foster child, they're exhausted and overwhelmed, just like all new parents. Several members of your church can visit a fix-and-freeze service such as Dream Dinners (dreamdinners.com) to assemble customized freezer meals for the family.

Throw a shower. Showers are one of the most meaningful ways members of your faith community can celebrate the arrival of a foster or adopted child. No matter what the child's age, gifts of clothing, age-appropriate toys, and other necessities are always appreciated. Children adopted as 'tweens and teens enjoy receiving gift cards or being taken on a shopping trip to the mall.

Chapter Five

How to Publicize Your Adoption Support Network

Shout it aloud, do not hold back. Raise your voice like a trumpet.

—Isaiah 58:1

*P*ublicizing your adoption support network requires ongoing effort. Studies show that people need exposure to a new product nine times before they remember it, so you must strategize multiple ways for people to experience your group.

Dedicate your ministry. If your church is your adoption network's home base, ask your pastor to dedicate your leadership team during a worship service. A dedication not only alerts the congregation of your ministry's existence, it assures them your pastoral leaders support your ministry.

Display information. Ask if you can present a brief verbal and/or electronic overview of your ministry during the dedication, in the bulletin, or after the service. When the service ends, greet people and invite them to learn more about your group. Display information and adoption resources on a table and encourage people to fill out an information sheet. Provide refreshments—or at the very least, a bowl of candy—goodies are always an irresistible draw.

Speak up. When we launched Heartbeat Ministries, I volunteered to share my journey through infertility and adoption in front of the congregation during the Sunday services. Our church has five services, each with close to 1,000 people in attendance. Plus a radio broadcast. I felt as if I was telling my story to the entire world!

The experience was scary, especially for an introvert like me. But I know people are most impacted by listening to someone's personal experience or testimony. During that two-minute (times five) spiel in front of the congregation, God gave me boldness and the courage to share from my heart.

If the idea of speaking in front of a large group causes you to break out in a cold sweat, ask your pastor to speak on your behalf. Or ask a church leader to interview you in front of the congregation. Structuring your presentation as an informal chat is more relaxing for you and for your listeners.

Your talk doesn't have to be a 45-minute or hour-long presentation, either. Try the following structures:

- 15-second prayer request
- 30-second announcement
- 2-minute Q & A
- Corporate prayer
- Reading a Bible passage that relates to adoption
- Introducing another person who will share his or her story

Teach. In addition to publicizing your network in front of the congregation, visit adult Sunday school classes and other venues in which you can interact with your audience.

When our church hosted a parenting conference, Heartbeat Ministries offered a workshop for parents-in-waiting. We arranged for eight panelists to share their infertility and adoption stories. While we expected a small turnout, only four people attended our workshop.

After our workshop my husband and I, feeling disheartened, headed to our church's gym for lunch. We introduced ourselves to the couple sitting next to us, and soon learned they were infertile. We encouraged them and handed them a stack of resource materials. Three months later, the couple adopted a baby boy. They e-mailed us the good news, saying, "Thank you for bringing us God's hope when we had none left."

Print Publicity

Within two months of launching Heartbeat Ministries, 50 people volunteered to become involved. My recruitment methods weren't the most conventional. One woman volunteered after I backed into her car in the church parking lot (unintentionally, of course). When I contacted her to pay the $900 damage I'd wreaked on her bumper, I learned she was a social worker in the perinatal unit of a local medical center. I immediately told her about our ministry, and she offered to help.

Another family (who'd heard me share my story during a church service) volunteered when I met them at the concession stand of a professional baseball game.

More conventional methods of publicizing your group include:

- Create a bulletin board that displays photos of your group's families, an events schedule, and testimonies about your network.
- Mail or e-mail picture postcards featuring families from your network.
- Prepare a brochure that identifies your mission, describes your network's various facets, contains an event calendar, and lists contact information. Distribute brochures in public locations that cater to your prospective clientele: adoption agencies, counseling offices, doctor's offices, pregnancy resource centers, and churches.
- Create a spreadsheet listing every adoption organization in your area. Contact each organization's publicist,

asking when their newsletter deadlines are so you can submit announcements in a timely manner. Notify publicists well in advance of any events your group hosts.

- Submit brief announcements about support groups, workshops, and other events to your local newspapers and parenting magazines. These publications often print community service announcements for free.
- Launch a Web site (see Chapter 4).
- Publish a quarterly newsletter or e-newsletter (see Chapter 4) that shares anecdotes, essays, and/or testimonies from group members. Send it to local churches, hospitals, pregnancy centers, counselors, and adoption organizations.
- Host a booth at a local adoption fair.

If your adoption network is church-based, utilize the church bulletin and newsletter. Here are some sample announcements you can adapt:

Adoption Support Network Launch

[Insert name of group]: This new ministry nurtures and supports pre-adoptive and post-adoptive families. We provide information and resources, one-to-one encouragement, small focus groups, fun, and fellowship [Insert contact information].

Infertility Support Group

Are you struggling to conceive or carry a pregnancy to term? You're not alone. Infertility effects one in every five couples. A new support group for couples facing fertility challenges meets [Insert information].

Birth Parent Support Group

Have you placed a child for adoption, either recently or years ago? Do you seek a supportive, Christ-centered group where you can discuss your feelings and work through post-adoption issues? You've found the right place [Insert information].

Workshop Series for Prospective Adoptive Parents

Thinking about adopting a child? Learn about the joys and trials of adoption during this 5-week series. Guest panelists will explain how to prepare for adopting a child, and they'll provide firsthand insights about various types of adoption.

Week 1: I want to adopt. Where do I start?

Week 2: International Adoption

Week 3: Domestic Open Adoption

Week 4: Special Needs and Foster-Adoption

Week 5: Preparing for Parenting

Dates:

Time:

Place:

Cost:

Childcare:

Registration:

Contact:

Individual Workshop Announcements
I Want to Adopt. Where Do I Start?

Can I love an adopted child as much as a biological child? Am I too old to adopt? What happens if an adoption fails? Confront your fears about adoption and have your questions about the adoption home study answered by several adoptive parents and a social worker from [X] Agency.

International Adoption

Learn about the unique aspects of adopting internationally and of becoming a multicultural family from parents who have adopted recently from [China, India, and Guatemala].

Open Adoption

Learn how to establish and maintain happy, healthy relationships with your child's birth family. Panelists at this session range from parents and birth parents who exchange letters and pictures to those who visit regularly with one another.

Special Needs and Foster-Adoption

Many parents adopt children who have physical or psychological challenges. Panelists at this session include [parents whose child has a cleft lip and palate and parents who adopted a child with Fetal Alcohol Syndrome through foster services].

Preparing for Parenting

Adoptive parents expend so much energy into bringing home their child that they often neglect to prepare for what happens next. During this workshop, several experienced parents will discuss issues that arise after adoption and will explain the dynamics of parenting both biological and adopted children.

Conclusion

God doesn't give us answers. He gives us himself.
　　　　—Frederick Buechner, pastor, author, theologian

I often hear from people who start an adoption support network in hopes of connecting with one or two others interested in adoption. They schedule a meeting and are flabbergasted when 30 people show up.

I also hear from people who expend a huge effort to launch their network and no one shows up. One woman told me, "I really worked on getting the word out about our meetings; I did an e-mail blitz and I had our pastor announce it during the service. But no one showed. I felt so discouraged and was at the point of giving up when someone called me, asking for information."

Adoption ministry is all about that single phone call—that single changed life. A successful adoption support network is forged through the partnership between you and God, as you allow God to shape you up for the task he has for you.[16] God will woo those who need to be part of your network. Whether that means one person or one hundred, faithfully serve those whom God sends your way.

Conclusion

May the love of the Lord Jesus draw you to himself; may the power of the Lord Jesus strengthen you in his service; may the joy of the Lord Jesus fill your soul.
>—William Temple, Archbishop of Canterbury from 1942–1944

Resources for Launching Your Network

Adoption by Grace (adoption-by-grace.com). Biblically-based support for adoptive families, professionals, and others who advocate for vulnerable children. Created by Phil Wong and Kristin Swick Wong (author of *Carried Safely Home*), the site offers print-and-use Bible studies that reflect on our adoption as God's children, passages about God's care for the fatherless, scriptures to help in decision-making, and links to sermons about adoption.

BirthMom Buds (birthmombuds.com). A peer support network of over 400 women worldwide who are considering adoption or who have placed children for adoption. Peer mentoring, monthly newsletter, and inspirational articles, as well as links for adoptive moms and adoption professionals.

Christianson, Laura. *The Adoption Decision: 15 Things You Want to Know Before Adopting.* Eugene, OR: Harvest House Publishers, 2007. This "how-to for the heart" helps prospective adoptive parents boldly confront their insecurities about adoption. The book thoroughly prepares them—and those in their support network—to welcome a child into their family. Includes study questions for group discussion as well as a chapter that explains the parallels between first-century Roman adoption practices, 21st century adoption practices, and our spiritual adoption into God's family. Laura's Web site (laurachristianson.com) offers a wealth of information and includes a database of adoption support networks worldwide.

Elizabeth Ministry International (elizabethministry.com/). Peer support, mentoring, spiritual nourishment, educational and inspirational resources for infertility, miscarriage, infant or child crisis, adoption and blended families, pregnancy, birth, and grandparents. 120 West 8th Street, Kaukauna, WI 54130; 920.766.9380.

FamilyLife's Hope for Orphans (familylife.com/hopefororphans/). Biblically-based information about adoption and orphan care. Free downloadable adoption information, resources for starting a church ministry for orphans, and one-day "If You Were Mine" adoption workshops in selected U.S. cities. 800-FL-TODAY.

Gillespie, Natalie Nichols. *Successful Adoption: A Guide for Christian Families.* Nashville, TN: Integrity Publishers, 2006. Chock-full of practical information, this book contains a chapter on starting an adoption or orphan care ministry.

Hannah's Prayer Ministries (hannahsprayer.org). Christian support and encouragement for couples worldwide who are struggling with fertility challenges, including primary and secondary infertility, pregnancy loss, early infant death and adoption loss. The ministry's outreach extends to those who become parents of living children through pregnancy, adoption, and/or foster care.

Heartlink (heartlink.org/). Focus on the Family's resource center for women in crisis pregnancy, with links to articles about adoption.

Home for Good Foundation (hfgf.org/). Christian ministry that encourages churches to empower families to adopt orphans and children living in foster care. Free downloadable PDFs by Gerald and Maureen Clark: "Starting and Growing Your Church Adoption Support Ministry: A Guide for

Leaders," and "Adoption, The Father Heart of God: An In-Depth Bible Study." 697 E. Intervale Rd., Grants Pass, OR 97527; 541.479.5926.

Jaynes, Sharon. *Building an Effective Women's Ministry: Develop a Plan, Gather a Team, Watch God Work.* Eugene, OR: Harvest House Publishers, 2005. Whether your women's ministry is thriving, struggling, or just starting out, this thorough, practical guide will help you build a ministry that women will be glad to call "home." Contains excellent resources for leadership team-building activities and suggestions for equipping leaders. Includes a chapter on starting an infertility ministry.

Kingdom Kids Adoption Ministries (kingdomkidsadoption.org). Equips people to care for orphans, provides resources and training about adoption and parenting, and helps families raise finances for adoption. Michelle Gardner's booklet, *The Ministry of Adoption,* describes the Scriptural basis for adoption and offers suggestions for how churches can minister to adoptive families. 1417 North Lincoln Street, Spokane, WA 99201; 509.465.3520.

LifeWay Christian Resources (lifeway.com/lwc/). Information and training in starting Christian support groups. Mic Morrow, One LifeWay Plaza, Nashville, TN 37234; 615.251.2816.

Presbyterians Pro-Life (ppl.org). An independent, non-profit corporation made up of members and pastors from the Presbyterian Church (U.S.A.), PPL has a crisis pregnancy ministry and offers a "God Gives Us Life Through Adoption" packet to help churches actively encourage and support adoption. The packet contains a poster, a pamphlet listing national adoption resources and a booklet for teenage girls experiencing crisis pregnancy. 3942 Middle Rd. Allison, Park, PA 15101; 415.487.1990.

Appendix: Resources for Launching Your Network

Project 1.27 (project127.com). An initiative of Transform Colorado, Project 1.27 is an excellent model of a community-based adoption network. Project 1.27 focuses on connecting Colorado foster children who are legally free for adoption with Christian adoptive families. While Project 1.27 is not an adoption agency, they assist families from the day they decide to adopt a child until at least six months after the adoption is completed. They arrange for support teams for each adoptive family, who assist with respite care, babysitting, and mentoring. Other families serve on prayer teams. Individuals also donate professional services to adoptive families: medical, dental, cleaning, technical, tutoring, and mechanical. Project 1.27: 2220 S. Chambers Rd., Aurora, CO 80014; 303.256.1225.

Shaohannah's Hope Foundation (shaohannahshope.org). Superb resources for church adoption ministries, including sermons on adoption, posters and handouts to help raise awareness of your adoption and orphan care ministry, and "Building a Bridge of H.O.P.E. Resource Guide," which includes a video for use at a church service to raise interest in adoption. Shaohannah's Hope also offers a free, downloadable resource, "Your Guide to Starting an Adoption Fund." The foundation also awards grants to qualified Christian families who are in the process of adopting. Shaohannah's Hope: 44180 Riverside Parkway, Lansdowne, VA, 20176; 800.784.5361.

Sikora, Pat. *Why Didn't You Warn Me?: How to Deal With Challenging Group Members.* Cincinnati, OH: Standard Publishing Company, 2007. Addresses 18 common problems well-meaning people create in small groups and provides step-by-step suggestions for dealing with them graciously and with sensitivity.

Stepping Stones (bethany.org/step). Christian ministry for couples facing fertility challenges or pregnancy loss. In addition to a newsletter, forums, and links to support groups, the ministry offers two helpful booklets: *Starting An Infertility Support Group* and *Without Hope, You are Hopeless!: A Bible Study for Couples Facing Fertility Challenges.* Bethany Christian Services, 901 Eastern Ave NE, PO Box 294, Grand Rapids, MI 49501; 616.224.7488.

Recommended Web Sites

Adoption.com. The Web's most popular adoption information destination for adoptive and foster families, women facing crisis pregnancy, and adopted people. Articles, blogs, message boards, chat rooms, waiting children photo listings, adoption profiles, adoption reunion registry, and "AdoptionWeek," the most widely circulated adoption e-zine. Adoption Media LLC, 459 North Gilbert Road, Suite C-100, Gilbert, AZ 85234; 480.446.0500.

AffordingAdoption.com. Links to grants, loans, employer benefits, and tips for fund-raising and saving money on adoption travel.

American Academy of Adoption Attorneys (AdoptionAttorneys.org). National association of attorneys who practice adoption law.

American Academy of Pediatrics Section on Adoption and Foster Care (aap.org/sections/adoption/). Nearly 200 medical professionals nationwide who provide care to and/or research health issues related to foster care and/or adoption.

Bulletin Board Services. WebsiteToolbox.com offers a free one-week trial and charges $5.00 per month after the trial period ends. Another service, MemberClicks.com, starts at $25 per month.

Chat Room Software. AddonChat.com lets you create a customizable chat room that runs directly from your Web site (they also offer a free version). To begin chatting, users simply type in a screen name of their choice and a password.

Child Welfare Information Gateway (childwelfare.gov/). Publications, statistics, and state statutes on all aspects of domestic and intercountry adoption.

Conference Call Services. FreeConferenceCall.com provides a (free) dedicated dial-in teleconferencing line for up to 96 callers per conference (callers pay long-distance charges). You can also record your call and distribute it free via RSS and podcasts.

Court Appointed Special Advocates (nationalcasa.org). CASA volunteers are trained to act as first-hand experts on the individual needs of abused and neglected children in foster care, giving them the best possible chance at a hopeful future.

DaveThomasFoundationForAdoption.org. Non-profit organization dedicated to increasing the adoptions of children in North America's foster care systems. 800.275.3832.

E-newsletter and E-zine Hosts. ConstantContact.com, VerticalResponse.com, CoolerEmail.com, iMakeNews.com, eZineDirector.com, AWeber.com.

Fund-raising Services. CafePress.com helps you create a variety of customized items for resale.

Life International (lifeintl.org)—Assists churches with launching and administering adoption funds. P.O. Box 40, 202 N. Ford St., Gridley, IL 61744; 309.747.3356.

Love Without Boundaries (lovewithoutboundaries.com). Humanitarian agency that sends volunteer medical teams to China, where they provide surgeries for orphans in hopes of increasing their chances of finding adoptive homes. Also sponsors foster care in China, nutrition programs, education programs, and adoption grant programs for orphans.

National Adoption Awareness Month Guide (nacac.org/resources). Free downloadable guide offers activities for commemorating Adoption Month, sample public service announcements, press releases, and more. The National Adoption Day site (nationaladoptionday.org) also provides a detailed tool kit to assist you in creating awareness and/or planning an event.

Network for Good (networkforgood.org). The largest non-profit charitable giving site provides a searchable database for users to donate to more than one million charities and search from among more than 36,000 volunteer opportunities. In addition, non-profits can access tools for fundraising, volunteer recruitment, and donor communication. They also let users create personalized charity badges that can be posted on blogs and Web sites to solicit funds for a particular charity.

Printing Services. VistaPrint.com has reasonable rates for printing business cards, postcards, stationery, and promotional products.

Shoes for Orphan Souls (shoesfororphansouls.org). Collects and distributes shoes to orphans in more than 44 countries. Includes tips for how to host a shoe drive.

Tapestry Books (tapestrybooks.com). Online bookstore specializing in the sale of adoption books.

Teleseminar Services. AudioAcrobat.com, which offers a 30-day free trial, allows you to record educational seminars, interviews, testimonials, radio shows, podcasts, video productions, and more by telephone or with your PC microphone. Vyew.com is a free teleconferencing service you can use in conjunction with FreeConferenceCall.com to host meetings, trainings, Q & A sessions, and workshops.

Yahoo! Groups (groups.yahoo.com). Discussion groups centered around all types and aspects of adoption.

Appendix: Resources for Launching Your Network

Organizations That Sponsor Humanitarian Missions

Buckner Orphan Care International (helporphans.org)
Children of Promise International (promise.org)
Children's HopeChest (hopechest.org/)
Global Aid Network (gainusa.org/)
Visiting Orphans (visitingorphans.org/)

Waiting Child Photo Listings

AdoptUSKids (adoptuskids.org). A tool for connecting foster and adoptive families with waiting children throughout the United States. Registration and participation on the site is free for homestudied families and foster adoption professionals. AdoptUSKids is a project of The Children's Bureau, part of the Federal Department of Health and Human Services.

RainbowKids.com. A monthly online international adoption magazine and the Internet's largest international adoption photo listing. P.O. Box 202, Harvey, LA 70059.

Adopting.com. Features U.S. and international waiting children photo listing, along with many other resources.

Endnotes

1. *Adoptive Families* magazine media kit.
2. Pertman, Adam, *Adoption Nation: How the Adoption Revolution is Transforming America* (Basic Books, 2001) and U.S. Children's Bureau, 2004.
3. U.S. Department of State, Bureau of Consular Affairs, and U.S. Children's Bureau, 2004.
4. U.S. Census Bureau, Census 2000.
5. The Dave Thomas Foundation for Adoption and The Evan B. Donaldson Adoption Institute, National Adoption Attitudes Survey, June 2002.
6. Barnes, Rebecca and Lowry, Lindy, "The American Church in Crisis," *Outreach* magazine, May/June 2006.
7. James 1:27.
8. Ephesians 1:6 NRSV.
9. John 15:17; Galatians 6:2.
10. Jaynes, Sharon, *Building an Effective Women's Ministry* (Harvest House Publishers, 2005), p. 251.
11. Psalm 35:5–6.
12. 1 Thessalonians 5:24.
13. Ephesians 6:18; 6:10.
14. Shaohannah's Hope, "Building a Bridge of H.O.P.E.: Starting Your Own Adoption or Orphan Care Ministry," p. 10 (*http://members.shaohannahshope. org/site/DocServer/SH_BuildingBridgesofHope_PDF. pdf?docID=121*).

15. FamilyLife Hope for Orphans, "Ten Ways Every Christian Can Care for the Orphan & Waiting Child" (*http://www.familylife.com/hopefororphans/TenWays_ inside.pdfA*).
16. 2 Timothy 3:17 MSG.

About The Author

Laura Christianson shares her passion for adoption with a worldwide audience through her award-winning "Exploring Adoption" blog. An adoptive mom, Laura founded Heartbeat Ministries, a Christian support network for adoptive families. She is the author of *The Adoption Decision* and is a popular speaker at adoption events and writers' conferences. Laura lives in Snohomish, Washington with her husband, Robert, and their two sons.

*If you are interested in having Laura speak at your event,
please visit:*

www.laurachristianson.com

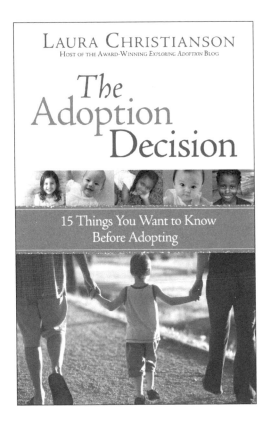

Are you interested in adopting but wonder whether you're up for the challenge? *The Adoption Decision* helps you work through your insecurities. Infused with dry humor, common-sense advice, biblical encouragement, and engaging vignettes from dozens of adoptive parents, this "how-to for the heart" will thoroughly prepare you—and those in your support net-work—to welcome your child with joy.

ISBN 978-0-7369-2000-1
U.S. $13.99
CAN $19.99
Harvest House Publishers

To order additional copies of this title call:
1-877-421-READ (7323)
or please visit our web site at
www.winepressbooks.com

If you enjoyed this quality custom published book,
drop by our web site for more books and information.

www.winepressgroup.com
"Your partner in custom publishing."